Contents

Introduction 3

DEATH 5

Because I Could Not Stop for Death 6
    Emily Dickinson

Death and the Woman 7
    Gertrude Atherton

The Lifted Veil Excerpt 13
    George Eliot

The Sinister Painting 19
    Greye La Spina

Sleeping At Last 34
    Christina Rossetti

THE UNCANNY 35

Superstition - An Ode 36
    Ann Radcliffe

The Evil Eye 37
    Lady Jane Wilde

Frankenstein Excerpt 46
    Mary Shelley

Contents continued...

Man-Size in Marble 53
  Edith Nesbit

Alien Boy 68
  Mary Darby Robinson

TORTURED LOVE 73

Demon Lovers 74
  Elinor Wylie

The Yellow Wallpaper 75
  Charlotte Perkins Gilman

The Were-Wolf 93
  Clemence Housman

The Striding Place 106
  Gertrude Atherton

Peregrine 113
  Elinor Wylie

Introduction

Silenced Shrieks is a collection of short stories, poems, and novel excerpts of horror stories written by female authors. In an era where men were the only credible authors capable of writing horror fiction, countless talented female authors' works were silenced and suppressed under the man's. In this anthology, some of the best-silenced works in horror fiction and poetry are showcased. The anthology is divided into three sections: death, the uncanny, and tortured lovers. When compiling the most intriguing works, all seemed to fall within one of the three horror sub-genres. Each of the sections begins and ends with a poem relating to its sub genre, and short stories and excerpts from novels fill in between.

The first section, "Death", contains texts with a chilling similarity: the death or murder of a character. This section contains works by Emily Dickinson, Gertrude Atherton, George Eliot, Greye La Spina, and Christina Rossetti. These authors' works were not given credibility, seeing that they were female authors, and even more specifically, female authors attempting to write in a historically male dominated field. George Eliot even went as far as changing her surname to sound like a man's to better her chance of publication. The texts contained in this first section showcase the darker side of horror fiction highlighting, in sometimes-graphic detail, the elements of murder.

The second section, "The Uncanny," includes texts with creepy, uncanny, and sometimes uncomfortable thematic elements. Texts contained in this section include works by Ann Radcliffe, Lady Jane Wilde, Mary Shelley, Edith Nesbit, and Mary Darby Robinson. These authors did a remarkable job of capturing the elements needed for horror fiction and were able to persevere in an unforgiving culture of successful men.

Finally, the third section, "Tortured Love," contains creepy texts about love gone wrong. Authors within this section include Elinor Wylie, Charlotte Perkins-Gilman, Clemence Housman, and Gertrude Atherton, all of who integrated love with a sinister twist in their writing. Love becomes entangled with madness derived from male dominance, mythical beasts, a missing friend or potential homoerotic lover, and journey to find redemption from sin. All of the works within this anthology are beautifully crafted and deserve to be praised for the authors' genius and bravery in publishing in an unacceptable era for women. These authors' works were silenced for too long, and now it has been our job to give voice to their "silenced shrieks."

Death

"Our dead are never dead to us, until we have forgotten them."
-George Eliot

This section includes works by Emily Dickinson, Gertrude Atherton, George Eliot, Greye La Spina, and Christina Rossetti. These women produced texts on the fatal side of horror, dealing with elements of death, murder, and disturbed post mortem experiences.

Because I Could Not Stop For Death

Emily Dickinson

Because I could not stop for Death –
He kindly stopped for me –
The Carriage held but just Ourselves –
And Immortality.

We slowly drove – He knew no haste
And I had put away
My labor and my leisure too,
For His Civility –

We passed the School, where Children strove
At Recess – in the Ring –
We passed the Fields of Gazing Grain –
We passed the Setting Sun –

Or rather – He passed us –
The Dews drew quivering and chill –
For only Gossamer, my Gown –
My Tippet – only Tulle –

We paused before a House that seemed
A Swelling of the Ground –
The Roof was scarcely visible –
The Cornice – in the Ground –

Since then – 'tis Centuries – and yet
Feels shorter than the Day
I first surmised the Horses' Heads
Were toward Eternity –

Death and the Woman

Gertrude Atherton

Her husband was dying, and she was alone with him. Nothing could exceed the desolation of her surroundings. She and the man who was going from her were in the third-floor-back of a

New York boarding-house. It was summer, and the other boarders were in the country; all the servants except the cook had been dismissed, and she, when not working, slept profoundly on the fifth floor. The landlady also was out of town on a brief holiday.

The window was open to admit the thick unstirring air; no sound rose from the row of long

narrow yards, nor from the tall deep houses annexed. The latter deadened the rattle of the

streets. At intervals the distant elevated lumbered protestinglyalong, its grunts and screams muffled by the hot suspended ocean.

She sat there plunged in the profoundest grief that can come to the human soul, for in all other agony hope flickers, however forlornly. She gazed dully at the unconscious breathing form of the man who had been friend, and companion, and lover, during five years of youth too vigorous and hopeful to be warped by uneven fortune. It was wasted by disease; the face was shrunken; the night-garment hung loosely about a body which had never been disfigured by flesh, but had been muscular with exercise and full-blooded with health. She was glad that the body was changed; glad that its beauty, too, had gone some other where than into the coffin.

She had loved his hands as apart from himself; loved their strong warm magnetism. They lay limp and yellow on the quilt: she knew that they were already cold, and that moisture was gathering on them. For a moment something convulsed within her. They had gone, too. She repeated the words twice, and, after them, "forever." And the while the sweetness of their pressure came back to her.

She leaned suddenly over him. He was in there still, somewhere. Where? If he had not ceased to breathe, the Ego, the Soul, the Personality was still in the sodden clay which had shaped to give it speech. Why could it not manifest itself to her? Was it still conscious in there, unable to project itself through the disintegrating matter which was the only medium its Creator had vouchsafed it? Did it struggle there, seeing her agony, sharing it, longing for the complete disintegration which should put an end to its torment? She called his name, she even shook him slightly, mad to tear the body apart and find her mate, yet even in that tortured moment realizing that violence would hasten his going.

The dying man took no notice of her, and she opened his gown and put her cheek to his heart, calling him again. There had never been more perfect union; how could the bond still be so strong if he were not at the other end of it? He was there, her other part; until dead he must be living. There was no intermediate state. Why should he be as entombed and un-responding as if the screws were in the lid? But the faintly beating heart did not quicken beneath her lips. She extended her arms suddenly, describing eccentric lines, above, about him, rapidly opening and closing her hands as if to clutch some escaping object; then sprang to her feet, and went to the window. She feared insanity. She had asked to be left alone with her dying husband, and she did not wish to lose her reason and shriek a crowd of people about her.

The green plots in the yards were not apparent, she noticed. Something heavy, like a pall, rested upon them. Then she understood that the day was over and that night was coming.

She returned swiftly to the bedside, wondering if she had remained away hours or seconds, and if he were dead. His face was still discernible, and Death had not relaxed it. She laid her own against it, then withdrew it with shuddering flesh, her teeth smiting each other as if an icy wind had passed.

She let herself fall back in the chair, clasping her hands against her heart, watching with expanding eyes the white sculptured face which, in the glittering dark, was becoming less defined of outline. Did she light the gas it would draw mosquitoes, and she could not shut from him the little air he must be mechanically grateful for. And she did not want to see the opening eye — the falling jaw.

Her vision became so fixed that at length she saw nothing, and closed her eyes and waited for the moisture to rise and relieve the strain. When she opened them his face had disappeared; the humid waves above the house-tops put out even the light of the stars, and night was come.

Fearfully, she approached her ear to his lips; he still breathed. She made a motion to kiss him, then threw herself back in a quiver of agony — hey were not the lips she had known, and she would have nothing less.

His breathing was so faint that in her half-reclining position she could not hear it, could not be aware of the moment of his death. She extended her arm resolutely and laid her hand on his heart. Not only must she feel his going, but, so strong had been the comradeship between them, it was a matter of loving honor to stand by him to the last.

She sat there in the hot heavy night, pressing her hand hard against the ebbing heart of the unseen, and awaited Death. Suddenly an odd fancy possessed her. Where was Death? Why was he tarrying? Who was detaining him? From what quarter would he come? He was taking his leisure, drawing near with footsteps as measured as those of men keeping time to a funeral march. By a wayward deflection she thought of the slow music that was always turned on in the theatre when the heroine was about to appear, or something eventful to happen. She had always thought that sort of thing ridiculous and inartistic. So had he.

She drew her brows together angrily, wondering at her levity, and pressed her relaxed palm against the heart it kept guard over. For a moment the sweat stood on her face; then the pent-up breath burst from her lungs. He still lived.

Once more the fancy wantoned above the stunned heart. Death — where was he? What a curious experience: to be sitting alone in a big house — she knew that the cook had stolen out — waiting for Death to come and snatch her husband from her. No; he would not snatch, he would steal upon his prey as noiselessly as the approach of Sin to Innocence — an invisible, unfair, sneaking enemy, with whom no man;s strength could grapple. If he would only come like a man, and take his chances like a man! Women had been known to reach the hearts of giants with the dagger's point. But he would creep upon her.

She gave an exclamation of horror. Something was creeping over the window-sill. Her limbs palsied, but she struggled to her feet and looked back, her eyes dragged about against her own volition. Two small green stars glared menacingly at her just above the sill; then the cat possessing them leaped downward, and the stars disappeared.

She realized that she was horribly frightened. "Is it possible?," she thought. "Am I afraid of Death, and of Death that has not yet come? I have always been rather a brave woman; He used to call me heroic; but then with him it was impossible to fear anything. And I begged them to leave me alone with him as the last of earthly boons. Oh, shame!"

But she was still quaking as she resumed her seat, and laid her hand again on his heart. She wished that she had asked Mary to sit outside the door; there was no bell in the room. To call would be worse than desecrating the house of God, and she would not leave him for one moment. To return and find him dead — gone alone!

Her knees smote each other. It was idle to deny it; she was in a state of unreasoning terror. Her eyes rolled apprehensively about; she wondered if she should see It when It came; wondered how far off It was now. Not very far; the heart was barely pulsing. She had heard of the power of the corpse to drive brave men to frenzy, and had wondered, having no morbid horror of the dead. But this! To wait — and wait — and wait — perhaps for hours — past the midnight — on to the small hours — while that awful, determined, leisurely Something stole nearer and nearer.

She bent to him who had been her protector with a spasm of anger. Where was the indomitable spirit that had held her all these years with such strong and loving clasp? How could he leave her? How could he desert her? Her head fell back and moved restlessly against the cushion; moaning with the agony of loss, she recalled him as he had been. Then fear once more took possession of her, and she sat erect, rigid, breathless, awaiting the approach of Death.

Suddenly, far down in the house, on the first floor, her strained hearing took note of a sound — a wary, muffled sound, as if someone were creeping up the stair, fearful of being heard.

Slowly! It seemed to count a hundred between the laying down of each foot. She gave a hysterical gasp. Where was the slow music?

Her face, her body, were wet — as if a wave of death-sweat had broken over them. There was a stiff feeling at the roots of her hair; she wondered if it were really standing erect. But she could not raise her hand to ascertain. Possibly it was only the coloring matter freezing and bleaching.

Her muscles were flabby, her nerves twitched helplessly.

She knew that it was Death who was coming to her through thesilent deserted house; knew that it was the sensitive ear of her intelligence that heard him, not the dull, coarse-grained ear of the body.

He toiled up the stair painfully, as if he were old and tired with much. work. But how could he afford to loiter, with all the work he had to do? Every minute, every second, he must be in demand to hook his cold, hard finger about a soul struggling to escape from its putrefying tenement. But probably he had his emissaries, his minions: for only those worthy of the honor did he come in person.

He reached the first landing and crept like a cat down the hall to the next stair, then crawled slowly up as before. Light as the footfalls were, they were squarely planted, unfaltering; slow; they never halted.

Mechanically she pressed her jerking hand closer against the heart; its beats were almost done.

They would finish, she calculated, just as those footfalls paused beside the bed.

She was no longer a human being; she was an Intelligence and an EarAR. Not a sound came from without, even the Elevated appeared to be temporarily off duty; but inside the big quiet house that footfall was waxing louder, louder, until iron feet crashed on iron stairs and echo thundered.

She had counted the steps — one — two — three — irritated beyond endurance at the long deliberate pauses between. As they climbed and clanged with slow precision she continued to count, audibly and with equal precision, noting their hollow reverberation. How many steps had the stair? She wished she knew.   No need! The colossal trampling announced the lessening distance in an increasing volume of sound not to be misunderstood. It turned the curve; it reached the landing; it advanced — slowly — down the hall; it paused before her door. Then knuckles of iron shook the frail panels. Her nerveless tongue gave no invitation. The knocking became more imperious; the very walls vibrated. The handle turned, swiftly and firmly. With a wild instinctive movement, she flung herself into the arms of her husband.

When Mary opened the door and entered the room she found a dead woman lying across a dead man.

The Lifted Veil Excerpt

George Eliot

When Meunier's visit was approaching its conclusion, there happened an event which caused some excitement in our household, owing to the surprisingly strong effect it appeared to produce on Bertha — on Bertha, the self-possessed, who usually seemed inaccessible to feminine agitations, and did even her hate in a self-restrained hygienic manner. This event was the sudden severe illness of her maid, Mrs. Archer. I have reserved to this moment the mention of a circumstance which had forced itself on my notice shortly before Meunier's arrival, namely, that there had been some quarrel between Bertha and this maid, apparently during a visit to a distant family, in which she had accompanied her mistress. I had overheard Archer speaking in a tone of bitter insolence, which I should have thought an adequate reason for immediate dismissal.

No dismissal followed; on the contrary, Bertha seemed to be silently putting up with personal inconveniences from the exhibitions of this woman's temper. I was the more astonished to observe that her illness seemed a cause of strong solicitude to Bertha; that she was at the bedside night and day, and would allow no one else to officiate as head-nurse. It happened that our family doctor was out on a holiday, an accident which made Meunier's presence in the house doubly welcome, and he apparently entered into the case with an interest which seemed so much stronger than the ordinary professional feeling, that one day when he had fallen into a long fit of silence after visiting her, I said to him — "Is this a very peculiar case of disease, Meunier?"

"No," he answered, "it is an attack of peritonitis, which will be fatal, but which does not differ physically from many other cases that have come under my observation. But I'll tell you what I have on my mind. I want to make an experiment on this woman, if you will give me permission. It can do her no harm — will give her no pain — for I shall not make it until life is extinct to all purposes of sensation. I want to try the effect of transfusing blood into her arteries after the heart has ceased to beat for some minutes. I have tried the experiment again and again with animals that have died of this disease, with astounding results, and I want to try it on a human subject. I have the small tubes necessary, in a case I have with me, and the rest of the apparatus could be prepared readily. I should use my own blood—take it from my own arm.

This woman won't live through the night, I'm convinced, and I want you to promise me your assistance in making the experiment. I can't do without another hand, but it would perhaps not be well to call in a medical assistant from among your provincial doctors. A disagreeable foolish version of the thing might get abroad."

"Have you spoken to my wife on the subject?" I said, "because she appears to be peculiarly sensitive about this woman: she has been a favourite maid."

"To tell you the truth," said Meunier, "I don't want her to know about it. There are always insuperable difficulties with women in these matters, and the effect on the supposed dead body may be startling. You and I will sit up together, and be in readiness.

When certain symptoms appear I shall take you in, and at the right moment we must manage to get everyone else out of the room."

I need not give our further conversation on the subject. He entered very fully into the details, and overcame my repulsion from them, by exciting in me a mingled awe and curiosity concerning the possible results of his experiment.

We prepared everything, and he instructed me in my part as assistant. He had not told Bertha of his absolute conviction that Archer would not survive through the night, and endeavoured to persuade her to leave the patient and take a night's rest. But she was obstinate, suspecting the fact that death was at hand, and supposing that he wished merely to save her nerves. She refused to leave the sick-room. Meunier and I sat up together in the library, he making frequent visits to the sick-room, and returning with the information that the case was taking precisely the course he expected. Once he said to me, "Can you imagine any cause of ill-feeling this woman has against her mistress, who is so devoted to her?"

"I think there was some misunderstanding between them before her illness. Why do you ask?"

"Because I have observed for the last five or six hours — since, I fancy, she has lost all hope of recovery — there seems a strange prompting in her to say something which pain and failing strength forbid her to utter; and there is a look of hideous meaning in her eyes, which she turns continually towards her mistress. In this disease the mind often remains singularly clear to the last."

"I am not surprised at an indication of malevolent feeling in her," I said. "She is a woman who has always inspired me with distrust and dislike, but she managed to insinuate herself into her mistress's favour." He was silent after this, looking at the fire with an air of absorption, till he went upstairs again. He stayed away longer than usual, and on returning, said to me quietly,

"Come now." I followed him to the chamber where death was hovering. The dark hangings of the large bed made a background that gave a strong relief to Bertha's pale face as I entered. She started forward as she saw me enter, and then looked at Meunier with an expression of angry inquiry; but he lifted up his hand as it to impose silence, while he fixed his glance on the dying woman and felt her pulse. The face was pinched and ghastly, a cold perspiration was on the forehead, and the eyelids were lowered so as to conceal the large dark eyes. After a minute or two, Meunier walked round to the other side of the bed where Bertha stood, and with his usual air of gentle politeness towards her begged her to leave the patient under our care — everything should be done for her — she was no longer in a state to be conscious of an affectionate presence. Bertha was hesitating, apparently almost willing to believe his assurance and to comply. She looked round at the ghastly dying face, as if to read the confirmation of that assurance, when for a moment the lowered eyelids were raised again, and it seemed as if the eyes were looking towards Bertha, but blankly. A shudder passed through Bertha's frame, and she returned to her station near the pillow, tacitly implying that she would not leave the room.

The eyelids were lifted no more. Once I looked at Bertha as she watched the face of the dying one. She wore a rich peignoir, and her blond hair was half covered by a lace cap: in her attire she was, as always, an elegant woman, fit to figure in a picture of modern aristocratic life: but I asked myself how that face of hers could ever have seemed to me the face of a woman born of woman, with memories of childhood, capable of pain, needing to be fondled? The features at that moment seemed so preternaturally sharp, the eyes were so hard and eager — she looked like a cruel immortal, finding her spiritual feast in the agonies of a dying race.

For across thosehard features there came something like a flash when the last hour had been breathed out, and we all felt that the dark veil had completely fallen. What secret was there between Bertha and this woman? I turned my eyes from her with a horrible dread lest my insight should return, and I should be obliged to see what had been breeding about two unloving women's hearts. I felt that Bertha had been watching for the moment of death as the sealing of her secret: I thanked Heaven it could remain sealed for me.

Meunier said quietly, "She is gone." He then gave his arm to Bertha, and she submitted to be led out of the room.

I suppose it was at her order that two female attendants came into the room, and dismissed the younger one who had been present before. When they entered, Meunier had already opened the artery in the long thin neck that lay rigid on the pillow, and I dismissed them, ordering them to remain at a distance till we rang: the doctor, I said, had an operation to perform — he was not sure about the death. For the next twenty minutes I forgot everything but Meunier and the experiment in which he was so absorbed, that I think his senses would have been closed against all sounds or sights which had no relation to it. It was my task at first to keep up the artificial respiration in the body after the transfusion had been effected, but presently Meunier relieved me, and I could see the wondrous slow return of life; the breast began to heave, the inspirations became stronger, the eyelids quivered, and the soul seemed to have returned beneath them. The artificial respiration was withdrawn: still the breathing continued, and there was a movement of the lips. Just then I heard the handle of the door moving: I suppose Bertha had heard from the women that they had been dismissed: probably a vague fear had arisen in her mind, for she entered with a look of alarm. She came to the foot of the bed and gave a stifled cry.

The dead woman's eyes were wide open, and met hers in full recognition — the recognition of hate. With a sudden strong effort, the hand that Bertha had thought forever still was pointed towards her, and the haggard face moved. The gasping eager voice said —

"You mean to poison your husband . . . the poison is in the black cabinet . . . I got it for you . . . you laughed at me, and told lies about me behind my back, to make me disgusting . . . because you were jealous . . . are you sorry . . . now?"

The lips continued to murmur, but the sounds were no longer distinct. Soon there was no sound — only a slight movement: the flame had leaped out, and was being extinguished the faster. The wretched woman's heart-strings had been set to hatred and vengeance; the spirit of life had swept the chords for an instant, and was gone again for ever. Great God! Is this what it is to live again . . . to wake up with our unstilled thirst upon us, with our unuttered curses rising to our lips, with our muscles ready to act out their half-committed sins?

Bertha stood pale at the foot of the bed, quivering and helpless, despairing of devices, like a cunning animal whose hiding-places are surrounded by swift-advancing flame. Even Meunier looked paralysed; life for that moment ceased to be a scientific problem to him. As for me, this scene seemed of one texture with the rest of my existence: horror was my familiar, and this new revelation was only like an old pain recurring with new circumstances.

The Sinister Painting
Greye La Spina

The taxi drove off, leaving Funk on the Hoddeston lawn, surrounded by valises. Funk was thinking it more than merely odd that Barclay, for whose coaching he had come prepared to spend a month, had not met him as planned. He tried the screen door; it was hooked inside.

"Hello, in there!" he hailed hopefully.

There was no response. The Hoddeston farm lay drenched in a torpid lethargy for which it was obvious more than the July heat must be responsible. Within the house, no one stirred. On the surrounding fields, no one was abroad. Even the usual sounds of the farm animals were hushed.

Funk was unpleasantly affected. Surely the entire household had not gone to meet his train and somehow missed it. He carried his traps to the stoop, crossed the yard to the barnyard, and halloed again. He knew of old where Barclay's studio was, so he set off down the path toward the grateful shade of the woods.

The gray stone walls of the old building soon glinted through the tree trunks and heavy foliage.
A strong conviction possessed Funk that Barclay was not within. In fact, he found the studio door padlocked. He noted that the west window was rudely boarded up. He walked around the studio to the north.

Here the trees had been cut down, and the studio wall was entirely of glass. He peered in with deepening curiosity, but apart from the usual litter of easels, painting paraphernalia and accessories, canvases in serried rows against the walls, his attention was almost immediately drawn to a painting propped against the south wall where the full light from the opposite windows poured in revealingly.

"Rum go!" Funk muttered, puzzled. "That never is Barclay's work. And he would never have let a student perpetrate such a monstrosity of line and crude color."

He pressed his face to the glass, cupping it against the outside light.

"That old man," Funk said aloud, amazed, "may be crudely done, but he's also absolutely horrible. His hands—ugh, they're dead hands. Bloodless—waxen—aaarrrgh! Something about the way he's sitting there—drooping as if he hadn't the strength of himself to sit erect, and was being held by something—something without, that you can't see. . . . I don't like the thing. It's ugly. There's—something wrong with it."

He said this last with conviction, and as he exclaimed became aware of another gaze fixed upon himself. He snapped upright and wheeled quickly. Waiting patiently for him to finish his examination of the studio's interior stood a man in patched, stained blue overalls.

"Well?" snapped Funk sharply, a bit taken aback.

"Mr. Barclay's at the house, sor. You're Mr. Funk? I'm Mulcahy, Hoddeston's hired man."

Funk nodded. "All right. I'm coming. How did Mr. Barclay come to miss my train?"

"We was all down to the police station, sor." Mulcahy fell in behind him.

"Police station?" echoed Funk. "What's been going on here?"

"I found Mr. Oakey dead in the studio this mornin', sor."

"What!" Funk whirled and confronted the Irishman.

"There's somethin' wrong in there, sor. I saw blood on the ould divil's beard." The man's voice quavered.

"Snap out of it, Mulcahy. Are you referring to that—picture?"

"I am that, sor."

"Blood on the old man's beard? Ridiculous! I saw none."

Mulcahy insisted stubbornly: "Blood it was, sor. An' the poor young man's was all drained out av him, sor."

Funk stiffened to deep attention. "Ha! This sounds

intriguing. Blood on the old man's beard?"

"An' drippin' from his dead fingers, sor. An' not wan dhrop left in the corpse, sor. Blood—all over the dommed ould divil's whiskers, an' his dead fingers, sor. Mary Mother!" Mulcahy crossed himself with pious haste.

"Who did that painting?" Funk demanded, turning again toward the house.

"A mon be the name av Silva, sor. He's afther bein' a cabinet-maker, but he got to thinkin' he cud paint, so he made that beauty back there, divil fly away wid him!"

"He sure can paint!" muttered Funk cryptically.

"He's mixin' somethin' wid his paint that only divils from the Pit can give him," the Irishman declared darkly. He hesitated, then rushed on: "Sor, the night before the poor lad was murthered, there was a fine canvas of Mr. Barclay's cut into ribbons, and Mr. Oakey's prize picture the same. What might that mean, along with the poor lad's bein' killed the next night? An' Silva only gettin' honorable mention last week, where he was lookin' for first prize?"

"Looks as if Silva had a motive," declared Funk as they walked into the barnyard.

Life was stirring normally about the farm now, as if a ban of enchanted silence had been lifted.

Funk could see Barclay's bulky body leaning over the valises on the front stoop. He hailed his friend, then asked Mulcahy hastily: "What do the police say?"

"Anny of us might have done it, sor, but the studio was locked from the inside. An' there's no motive. An' they can't figure where the poor lad's blood wint, sor." Back of the simple words pushed a dark significance of terrible things.

"Looks as if there were more here than appears on the surface."

"Right you are, sor. From now on, Tom Mulcahy wears a blessed medal next his hide, day an' night."

Funk met Barclay's welcoming hand with a heartening grip.

"Sorry to have missed you, Funk, but this ghastly

tragedy has dislocated all plans. I—I was fond of the boy," groaned Barclay, his face working. "He had a gift, had Harry. I—I was looking forward to what he would do with color in the not far future. And now——" his voice broke.

"Where's my room, Barclay?" Funk gathered up his bags and followed the other painter up the front stairs.

Both men lighted cigarettes in silence. Barclay stared abstractedly from the window, while Funk unpacked rapidly, puffing clouds of smoke about himself as he tossed shirts, underwear, ties, into the open bureau drawers.

"I want to know how Silva's painting got into your studio," he said at last, with an air of relief as he finished his work.

"So you are taking that attitude?" Barclay asked, his eyes heavy.

Funk did not attempt to evade the implied issue. "Anybody but a crass, materialistic jackass would," he responded quietly.

"I didn't know you went in for that sort of thing. I've no time for anything but painting. Just making a living takes most of my time these days, Funk."

The younger man's eyes snapped. "A very little suffices for me. I'm too fascinated with studying the truths underlying the illusions of material existence. Not that I've gotten very far, but what I know, I know."

"Then perhaps you can say what's unnatural about poor Harry's death? I know there's—something wrong about it."

"Something wrong!" echoed the younger man thoughtfully.

"Yes, there's something wrong—and uncanny—about this lad's death. As to its being unnatural, there are many strange and little-known laws operating along lines so new to us——" He broke off there, his expression clearing as if an illuminating idea had suddenly clarified the situation for him. "I believe the poor chap's death is due to an extremely interesting example of the transference of an evil will-to-power."

Barclay wheeled from the window, saying abruptly: "I didn't tell the police what I felt lay behind this tragedy. I have no hankering to live in an insane asylum. Now I have a faint hope that you may be able to appreciate the strangeness of my experience. Listen!

"Manuel Silva settled here a few years ago and has been doing well as a cabinetmaker. Recently he learned that I got from three hundred dollars up, for a canvas. He thought this an easy way to get rich, but I refused to teach him. You know, I never take any but advanced students of decided promise. My refusal roused Silva's furious resentment.

"I have instituted an annual art exhibit in town. Silva entered three canvases, to force my hand. They were rather terrible. One was a blacksmith, dark, sullen, sinister; he was hammering viciously at what appeared to be a battered crucifix. Another was a farmer slaughtering a wretched hog that somehow looked like a naked man; the butcher's face wore a too realistic grin of sadistic enjoyment as he wielded his bloody knife. The third—the third was the painting you've just seen in my studio.

"Harry's entry took first prize; this was inevitable. I felt inclined to encourage a couple of young local artists, so gave them honorable mention. Not to slight Silva's pride, I included him.

"The night before the canvases were removed, Harry and I were in the gallery, and he pointed out that someone had deliberately cut the honorable mention ribbon on Silva's canvas so that it hung in dangling strips. Odd, that, eh?"

"You're opening vistas," replied Funk, lighting another cigarette from the one he had been smoking. "You are absorbingly interesting."

"I criticized Silva's painting, observing that Harry was right when he said it gave him the jitters, but that in just that degree it possessed a touch of wild genius. Harry pronounced it ghastly, to paint a hunched-up old man as dead as a doornail, his hands frightful, decomposing—yet sitting up there—ugh! Silva's colors were crude, his drawing distorted—just how, it would be difficult to say, but—wrong, you understand—wrong.

"I said I dared not encourage Silva because of a very strange quality in his work—that something wrong. And then we both nearly jumped out of our skins, for in the dusk behind us someone broke into an ugly chuckle, and we turned to see a dark figure slouching out. It was Silva, and I realized that he'd heard me pronounce him an evil genius. Harry made light of my compunctions, but I was disturbed.

"We confronted the old man in the painting once more. As twilight gained the room, a murky dusk seemed creeping into the very canvas. Its shadows deepened. The old man merged into his dark background; all but his pallid face, his grayish beard, the waxen fingers dropping over his angular knees. It was wrong. Entirely wrong. And then all at once Harry twitched my sleeve, and exclaimed, 'Let's get out of here!' and we turned and plunged into the street, stricken by some subtle panic so obsessing that it was not until we were back at the Hoddeston farm that we realized how foolish and unreasonable had been our flight."

Funk lighted another cigarette.

"We went sketching next day," Barclay went on, "and Hoddeston brought our canvases back to the studio. That night he told me that Silva had sent me one of his for a gift; so Harry and I went down to see which one. We lighted candles, and really, we got a nasty shock. The flickering, inadequate candle-light made that old man appear more than ever an entity with a horrid existence independent of his painted presentment. Harry said, 'My God!' in a kind of comic dismay.

"I knew instinctively that Silva was up to no good; he bore me malice. His very gift seemed to convey dire menace. In the pale candle-light the old man's beard appeared to rustle stiffly as if his lips were parting under its bushy shelter. Of course, I could not see anything, but I felt that I was seeing a pale dead tongue flick moisture over dry dead lips. Ugh!"

"That must have been an odd sensation," cogitated Funk aloud, as he expelled a thick cloud of smoke. "You make it very clear."

"Yes? Well, there's more of it, Funk. Oakey and I went over our canvases to check on their return and good condition. We were satisfied. Just remember this point, will you? We padlocked the studio door and went off to bed. When we went in next morning, the padlock was undisturbed, and all the windows locked on the inside.

"But one of my best canvases had been slit into ribbons. And Harry's, which had taken first prize, was completely demolished, even the frame. That last act of vandalism made me feel bad. I'd been sure the boy could cash in on his work, and he needed the money. He took it like a Spartan, but he told me he was going to sleep in the studio that night, for he felt sure that Silva had done the damage.

"I agreed, although I couldn't figure out how Silva could have gotten inside. So last night I left the boy there. He said he was going to hang something over the old man's gosh-awful face. I offered to stay with him, but he wouldn't have it. This morning—" Barclay broke down, turning back to the window with a suspicious gulp.

"Mulcahy told me," Funk hastened to say, lighting another cigarette.

"It was ghastly, Funk. Mulcahy was howling 'Blood!' at every jump he took. Blood, he yelled, on the old man's beard!"

"H'm. How about the coroner?"

"Harry'd been dead for hours. Finger marks on his throat Every drop of blood drained from his body," Barclay said with slow emphasis. "Mulcahy had seen him through the north windows. I had to break the west window to get in. The coroner said at first that he'd had a fit but finally decided he'd been killed by a person unknown."

"About the blood?" queried Funk.

"Mulcahy was right about it. Funk—I saw it, too."

"It's not there now," Funk declared.

Barclay nodded. "That's another strange thing. When I rushed over, I found poor Harry sprawling on the floor, his body all twisted in a grotesque, gruesome position. And so terribly white! As I threw myself on the floor beside him, something struck upon my inner ear. It was a sound. But such a sound! Even as I heard it, I knew I was hearing what could not be apprehended physically.

"I sprang to my feet and confronted Silva's hideous canvas. God, it was horrible!" He shuddered at the bare recollection. "The painted old man sat there motionless, but it was a sinister restraint, Funk. I stared, stricken by a horror that affected me with nausea, for I saw then that someone had smeared that ancient's deathly pallor with crimson that crawled down the painted gray beard. The dead hands that hung over the angular knees were dripping, every pallid finger-tip, with blood. Blood, Funk!"

"How do you know it was blood?" Funk demanded sharply.

"I—I touched it," whispered the old man, distastefully.

"And then?" Funk prompted, not ungently.

"A ghastly thing came to pass. I did not see it. I felt, rather than saw. I became aware with that inner sense of the movement of one of the old man's painted arms. It lifted with the jerking unevenness of an automaton, and passed across the stained gray beard. I say, it moved. I felt it move, yet at the same time I was aware that it was only painted, hence incapable of movement. It was a Something Else behind it that actually moved.

"I find it almost impossible to clarify my intuitions," Barclay deprecated despairingly, "other than to say that while the painted figure did not stir, I was yet inwardly aware that it lifted one arm and wiped away the crimson from its beard. Then it reached out on either side, to drag off that horrible drip from its waxen finger-tips against the painted grass that reddened under them.

"God! It was the more horrible because, although the figure did not show movement to my straining eyes, yet I saw the crimson life-blood of poor Harry disappearing from the canvas as those movements which I felt, rather than saw, took place. Of course this explanation is inadequate," he finished.

Funk pushed the consumed tip of his cigarette to the

fresh one he was holding between his thin lips. A cloud of blue smoke enveloped him, out of which his voice pronounced decidedly:

"Not inadequate, my dear fellow. On the contrary, it is very enlightening; so clear that I believe we may yet punish the murderer of that poor lad."

Barclay's dreamy eyes burned with sudden fire. "I'd give a year of my life to accomplish that," he exclaimed fiercely.

"I hardly think so much will be required, but you may have to sacrifice one or two of your canvases. We'd better get the rest of Oakey's work over here. And Silva must learn that you are taking steps to protect Harry's work and your own. He must be informed that tomorrow night you yourself will sleep in the studio. That will bring him," Funk predicted darkly.

"You agree that it's Silva!" cried Barclay in relief.

"I've no doubt of it. But not in propria persona. He's projecting his astral body through that hideous old man, and he's already made a grave error."

"What do you mean?"

"He's permitted himself to savor human blood. Hence, he can not be permitted to—continue.

He's dangerous, now. He will be yet more so, unless checked. I propose to do this in the only permanent way possible."

"We have no proof of his presence in the studio, Funk. Who would believe the intangible evidence of my experience?"

"No one, ordinarily," Funk agreed, adding quickly, "but I believe. And there is another person who will not only believe, but will furnish me with the means of putting a stop to Silva's murderous proclivities, without disturbing the authorities unduly," he finished dryly.

"Wouldn't it be wise to return that picture to Silva? Or cut it to bits and burn it?" suggested Barclay uneasily.

"Later," said Funk, queerly. "You see, Silva has somehow learned how to transfer his will-for-evil to that creature of his own making. It is through that same creation that we must reach him and stop his criminal career before it is too late."

Barclay sighed. "You speak as if you knew what you were talking about, Funk. I can't just understand you, but I feel that you are somehow right. What do you wish done?"

"Get Mulcahy—or Hoddeston—to clear out all Oakey's canvases. Leave only a couple of your own that you don't particularly care about, so as not to stir Silva's suspicions overly. He'll imagine you're exhibiting. Then have Hoddeston step in and tell Silva what happened to the canvases in the studio, and ask him to have his moved out of harm's way. That will appear a kindly impulse on your part, and he will reply that he'll send for his canvas in a couple of days. He'll figure on polishing you off by then," finished Funk callously.

"Agreeable thought, that," sighed the older painter.

"Now, you're going to lend me your roadster. I'll be back tomorrow afternoon at the latest. Be sure Silva is given to understand that tomorrow night you'll be sleeping in the studio. Under no circumstances, however, venture in there tonight," Funk warned gravely. "Tonight Silva, or whatever wakens in the studio under the stimulus of his evil purpose, may have free play. But tomorrow night—ah, tomorrow night I shall be there, not you."

"I won't permit your getting into a nasty situation, Funk. This isn't your affair, after all. Harry was my protegé. It's up to me."

"Are you prepared to give effective battle to a painted demon, Barclay?" Funk's laugh was incredulous. "Can you, through that painted thing, silence for ever the intangible, distant malefactor?"

"You can do such things?" said Barclay's hushed murmur.

"I shall know how to, before I return tomorrow afternoon."

"But how?"

"I'm going to someone who knows. I shall demand the secret. She will yield it, I am certain. I'm going to see Gwen Carradorne."

"Where have I heard that name?" puzzled Barclay.

"Possibly in connection with her published brochures.

Her Reality of the Abstract is fairly well known; it's discussed everywhere."

"Quite likely," sighed Barclay. "I seem to remember it vaguely."

"Now," pursued Funk briskly, "how about your car?"

It was dusk when Funk returned on the following day. The seriousness and abstraction that wove a cloak about him struck Barclay's curious inquiries into silence. A certain high air about the younger artist forbade imperiously any break upon that lofty mood. Funk's first query was, Had Silva been duly informed of the occupation of the studio that night?

"He knows. He told Hoddeston that he would call for his unappreciated masterpiece in a couple of days." The words were significantly emphasized.

"I rather fancied he'd say that. He knows you'll be there tonight?"

"Hoddeston told him, if there were any further trouble, I'd sleep there from tonight on, to protect his painting."

"Excellent!" Funk rubbed his hands together and blew a cloud of thick smoke from the cigarette in one corner of his mouth. "And was there any?"

"Yes. Last night the two canvases I'd left were demolished."

"Good! He'll be expecting you to sleep there tonight. Let's have supper. Then I'll run into town and fetch Miss Carradorne. She insists upon coming out; the time was too brief to prepare me to handle the situation single-handed."

"That's extraordinarily kind of her, Funk. But if she is to be at the studio tonight, why not I?" Barclay insisted.

"She would have handled it alone, only that she—"

Funk broke off suddenly, looking apologetic. "Sorry I can't be more explicit, but she bans discussion of herself unless she decides to come out into the open, which she rarely does. She's—well, wait until you meet her, if she permits it," Funk broke off, in a kind of embarrassment. "You'll understand then. But believe me, she is worthy the highest respect and admiration a human being could expect."

Funk did not have to drive to town. Between dusk and dark a shining dark blue car with a special delivery body slipped into the driveway. From the limousine-like front two uniformed men alighted and walked to the rear of the car. There were wide doors there, which they proceeded to open. They withdrew, with the utmost care, a strange anachronism; a blue-and-black-and-gold decorated sedan chair, small and delicate. They placed themselves between the shafts and started toward the farmhouse.

Funk exclaimed, and sprang down the steps to meet that odd equippage. He bent over what was obviously an extended hand, white in the dusk. Barclay, staring, saw the young artist touch his lips to those extended fingers. A child's high, shrilly sweet voice gave an order, and the chair-bearers carried the sedan chair toward the barnyard. Funk followed, calling back as he went.

"See you tomorrow morning, Barclay." With that, he disappeared after the chair into the soft darkness beyond the barnyard.

Barclay felt that he could not sleep. He was intensely irritated that Gwen Carradorne should have sent a child to take her place in what he felt must be a post of danger. He went down to the shining automobile and walked around it with curiosity. The rear doors had been closed, and nothing marked it as out of the ordinary save, perhaps, the expensive type of shock-absorbers for a delivery body; and of course, what looked very like a periscope set in the top, as much out of place as was a modern child in a sedan chair.

He sat at his window, fell asleep there in his chair, and did not waken until Mrs. Hoddeston tapped at his door, calling that Mr. Funk and the little girl had returned. She volunteered that the little girl was a perfect little French doll.

Barclay took the stairs three at a stride. In the hall Funk sat on a hassock which brought his face slightly below the level of the small oval countenance of the child, who sat sedately on the hall chair.

Barclay noted with an artist's appreciation the bloom on

her dazzling cheeks; the straight nose; the richly scarlet mobile lips. He approved the curling black lashes, finely penciled arching eyebrows, sleek black bobbed hair. Her creamy silk dress, rather longer than worn by most children of her age (apparently about six), was smocked in a knowing fashion with bright colors.

Her feet were inappropriately encased in high-heeled French slippers.

All this the artist in Barclay captured at a glance, just as he took in the beauty of the slender, tiny hands, of the taper fingers, and the eloquence of every gesture. A strange, an unusual child, this. His leaping footsteps brought upon him a lifting of fringed eyelids, and what he felt shrinkingly was a glance of indifference. He stopped short at the foot of the staircase, abashed at this disdainful glance.

He knew all at once why this child's frock was longer than customary; why her tiny feet wore adult-styled foot-gear; why sophistication animated those taper fingers. The cobalt blue eyes that regarded him from the child's elfin face were the eyes of a grown woman. They were the informed eyes of one who has passed through the fires of varied experiences; the eyes of one who has gazed unafraid upon unveiled mysteries. The child was not a child, but was an exquisite midget, a creature set apart from the entire world by her miniature proportions.

Funk sprang up, caught the other man's hand and drew him down to the hassock, himself sinking upon the floor so that both men's faces were below the level of the midget's.

"Barclay," Funk said, in a tone of repressed excitement, "Miss Carradorne permits me to present you."

"Honored, Miss Carradorne," mumbled Barclay, still confused under the keen gaze of those faintly derisive blue eyes. He understood it, after a minute; she was touched with amusement at his discomfiture.

An elfish smile twitched at one corner of her scarlet lips, and she actually turned away those too-shrewd eyes as if to spare Barclay's feelings, a kindly gesture which did not serve to tranquillize him, for there was just a touch of condescension in her half-smile.

"Mr. Funk has been showing me these canvases from your studio," she said, slowly, in a shrilly sweet voice. "I would very much like that snow scene; it is charming. If you will tell me the price—?"

Barclay's embarrassment vanished. Here he could be sure of himself.

"I would feel honored if you would accept it as a proof of my gratitude for your having come here," he began, but his eyes questioned Funk.

"You are anxious to learn the outcome of last night's plans?" said Miss Carradorne's high voice lightly.

Suspended in the bosom of her frock by a slender platinum chain was a platinum whistle which she put to her lips and sounded. At once the bearers of the sedan chair came up the steps and into the hall, holding the chair close to their mistress. Like some bright bird, so airy and graceful was her lithe movement, she seemed to fly from her chair into the sedan's shelter. She waved one tiny hand. The bearers took their light burden outside, slid it into place in the rear of the waiting automobile. They mounted into the front, and the car slipped noiselessly away down the road, bespeaking the many-cylindered motor by its very silence and power.

Barclay stared after it, amazed. "So that strange little thing is your wonderful Gwen Carradorne? Why didn't you warn me?"

Funk lighted a cigarette hastily and began surrounding himself with smoke. "Why didn't I?
Because she won't be talked about. She's proud and sensitive. She considers her miniature body the ultimate of human perfection, and won't permit its comparison with what she considers our gross bodies. And she's abnormally proud of her brain. She has reason to be. I think it is the most highly developed I have ever known. As an occultist—she's the seventh daughter of a seventh daughter—"

Funk broke off bruskly. "You are anxious to know about

last night? She has forbidden me to divulge details, but I may tell you briefly that Silva will never again repeat his evil act."

"He was there, then, last night?" gasped Barclay incredulously.

"Not in propria persona, but his familiar was already locked in with us, when I bolted the door behind Gwen and myself."

"What do you mean?"

Funk sighed resignedly. "Let's go down to the studio. It's easier to understand, when you've seen things with your own eyes."

The telephone rang. Mrs. Hoddeston ran out of the kitchen and answered it. An expression of horror settled on her placid face.

"Manuel Silva's been found dead, with a knife-wound in his throat," she called, and gave closer attention to the telephone.

Funk beckoned Barclay silently, and the two hurried across the barnyard and into the woods. With the key Barclay had loaned him, Funk unlocked the padlock. He pushed the studio door open. Words seemed superfluous.

Spread on the floor lay a painted canvas figure, pinned down by a knife through its throat. The edges of the canvas were sharply defined as if just cut out of the painting leaning against the south wall with a neatly trimmed vacancy in its center.
Barclay stared, closed his eyes convulsively, then stared again.

"I couldn't have done it alone," Funk kept repeating in a kind of feverish excitement. "She furnished the power. She'd have done it herself, but she's too—I mean," he corrected himself hastily, "he was too tall."

Barclay stared, motionless. He was absorbing the details of a bizarre thing which confirmed him in his hasty resolution to burn Silva's painting without delay.

The empty space in the painting distinctly outlined a drooping, seated figure. The painted canvas shape lying on the floor, pinned down by the knife through its pallid painted throat, could have filled that vacancy twice over.
It was a full length, standing figure. . . .

Sleeping at Last

Christina Rossetti

Sleeping at last, the trouble and tumult over,
Sleeping at last, the struggle and horror past,
Cold and white, out of sight of friend and of lover,
Sleeping at last.

 No more a tired heart downcast or overcast,
No more pangs that wring or shifting fears that hover,
Sleeping at last in a dreamless sleep locked fast.

 Fast asleep.
 Singing birds in their leafy cover
Cannot wake her, nor shake her the gusty blast.

Under the purple thyme and the purple clover
Sleeping at last.

THE UNCANNY

"The silence depressed me. It wasn't the silence of
silence. It was my own silence."
- Sylvia Plath, *The Bell Jar*

This selection of texts by Ann Radcliffe,
Lady Jane Wilde , Mary Shelley, Edith Nesbit, and
Mary Darby Robinson includes creepy thematic
elements on the spectrum of horror fiction.
Straying away from conventional, blatant uses of
horrific elements, these authors chose to write in a
way that is chilling to the core.

Superstition- An Ode

Ann Radcliffe

High mid Alverna's awful steeps,
Eternal shades, and silence dwell,
Save, when the gale resounding sweeps,
Sad straings are faintly heard to swell:

Enthron'd amid the wild impending rocks,
Involv'd in clouds, and brooding future woe,
The demon Superstition Nature shocks,
And waves her Sceptre o'er the world below.

Around her throne, amid the mingling glooms,
Wild-hideous forms are slowly seen to glide;
She bids them fly to shade earth's brightest blooms,
And spread the blast of Desolation wide.

See! in the darkened air their fiery course!
The sweeping ruin settles o'er the land,
Terror leads on their steps with madd'ning force,
And Death and Vengeance close the ghastly band!

Mark the purple streams that flow!
Mark the deep empassioned woe!
Frantic Fury's dying groan!
Virtue's sigh, and Sorrow's moan!

Wide-wide the phantoms swell the loaded air
With shrieks of anguish-madness and despair!
Cease your ruin! spectrs dire!
Cease your wild terrific sway!
Turn your steps-and check your ire,
Yield to peace and mourning day!'

The Evil Eye
Lady Jane Wilde

There is nothing more dreaded by the people, nor considered more deadly in its effects, than the Evil Eye.

It may strike at any moment unless the greatest precautions are taken, and even then there is no true help possible unless the fairy doctor is at once summoned to pronounce the mystic charm that can alone destroy the evil and fatal influence.

There are several modes in which the Evil Eye can act, some much more deadly than others. If certain persons are met the first thing in the morning, you will be unlucky for the whole of that day in all you do. If the evil-eyed comes in to rest, and looks fixedly on anything, on cattle or on a child, there is doom in the glance; a fatality which cannot be evaded except by a powerful counter-charm. But if the evil-eyed mutters a verse over a sleeping child, that child will assuredly die, for the incantation is of the devil, and no charm has power to resist it or turn away the evil. Sometimes the process of bewitching is effected by looking fixedly at the object, through nine fingers; especially is the magic fatal if the victim is seated by the fire in the evening when the moon is full. Therefore, to avoid being suspected of having the Evil Eye, it is necessary at once, when looking at a child, to say "God bless it." And when passing a farmyard where the cows are collected for milking, to say, "The blessing of God be on you and on all your labours." If this form is omitted, the worst results may be apprehended, and the people would be filled with terror and alarm, unless a counter-charm were not instantly employed.

The singular malefic influence of a glance has been felt by most persons in life; an influence that seems to paralyze intellect and speech, simply by the mere presence in the room of someone who is mystically antipathetic to our nature. For the soul is like a fine-toned harp that vibrates to the slightest external force or movement, and the presence and glance of some persons can radiate around us a divine joy, while others may kill the soul with a sneer or a frown. We call these subtle influences mysteries, but the early races believed them to be produced by spirits, good or evil, as they acted on the nerves or the intellect.

Some years ago an old woman was living in Kerry, and it was thought so unlucky to meet her in the morning, that all the girls used to go out after sunset to bring in water for the following day, that so they might avoid her evil glance; for whatever she looked on came to loss and grief.

There was a man, also, equally dreaded on account of the strange, fatal power of his glance; and so many accidents and misfortunes were traced to his presence that finally the neighbours insisted that he should wear a black patch over the Evil Eye, not to be removed unless by request; for learned gentlemen, curious in such things, sometimes came to him to ask for a proof of his power, and he would try it for a wager while drinking with his friends.

One day, near an old ruin of a castle, he met a boy weeping in great grief for his pet pigeon, which had got up to the very top of the ruin, and could not be coaxed down.

"What will you give me," asked the man, "if I bring it down for you?"

"I have nothing to give," said the boy, "but I will pray to God for you. Only get me back my pigeon, and I shall be happy."

Then the man took off the black patch and looked up steadfastly at the bird; when all of a sudden it fell to the ground and lay motionless, as if stunned; but there was no harm done to it, and the boy took it up and went his way, rejoicing.

A woman in the County Galway had a beautiful child, so handsome, that all the neighbours were very careful to say "God bless it" when they saw him, for they knew the fairies would desire to steal the child, and carry it off to the hills.

But one day it chanced that an old woman, a stranger, came in. "Let me rest," she said, "for I am weary." And she sat down and looked at the child, but never said "God bless it." And when she had rested, she rose up, looked again at the child fixedly, in silence, and then went her way.

All that night the child cried and would not sleep. And all next day it moaned as if in pain. So the mother told the priest, but he would do nothing for fear of the fairies. And just as the poor mother was in despair, she saw a strange woman going by the door. "Who knows," she said to her husband, "but this woman would help us." So they asked her to come in and rest. And when she looked at the child she said "God bless it," instantly, and spat three times at it, and then sat down.

"Now, what will you give me," she said, "if I tell you what ails the child?"

"I will cross your hand with silver," said the mother, "as much as you want, only speak," and she laid the money on the woman's hand. "Now tell me the truth, for the sake and in the name of Mary, and the good Angels."

"Well," said the stranger, "the fairies have had your child these two days in the hills, and this is a changeling they have left in its place. But so many blessings were said on your child that the fairies can do it no harm. For there was only one blessing wanting, and only one person gave the Evil Eye. Now, you must watch for this woman, carry her into the house and secretly cut off a piece of her cloak. Then burn the piece close to the child, till the smoke as it rises makes him sneeze; and when this happens the spell is broken, and your own child will come back to you safe and sound, in place of the changeling."

Then the stranger rose up and went her way.

All that evening the mother watched for the old woman, and at last she spied her on the road.

"Come in," she cried, "come in, good woman, and rest, for the cakes are hot on the griddle, and supper is ready."

So the woman came in, but never said "God bless you kindly," to man or mortal, only scowled at the child, who cried worse than ever.

Now the mother had told her eldest girl to cut off a piece of the old woman's cloak, secretly, when she sat. down to eat. And the girl did as she was desired, and handed the piece to her mother, unknown to anyone. But, to their surprise, this was no sooner done than the woman rose up and went out without uttering a word; and they saw her no more.

Then the father carried the child outside, and burned the piece of cloth before the door, and held the boy over the smoke till he sneezed three times violently: after which he gave the child back to the mother, who laid him in his bed, where he slept peacefully, with a smile on his face, and cried no more with the cry of pain. And when he woke up the mother knew that she had got her own darling child back from the fairies, and no evil thing happened to him any more.

The influence of the mysterious and malign power of the Evil Eye has at all times been as much dreaded in Ireland as it is in Egypt, Greece, or Italy at the present day. Everything young, beautiful, or perfect after its kind, and which naturally attracts attention and admiration, is peculiarly liable to the fatal blight that follows the glance of the Evil Eye. It is therefore an invariable habit amongst the peasantry never to praise anything without instantly adding, "God bless it;" for were this formula omitted, the worst consequences would befall the object praised.

The superstition must be of great antiquity in Ireland, for Balor, the Fomorian giant and hero, is spoken of in an ancient manuscript as able to petrify his enemies by a glance; and how ho became possessed of the power is thus narrated:—

One day as the Druids were busy at their incantations, while boiling a magical spell or charm, young Balor passed by, and curious to see their work, looked in at an open window. At that moment the Druids happened to raise the lid of the caldron, and the vapour, escaping, passed under one of Balor's eyes, carrying with it all the venom of the incantation. This caused his brow to grow to such a size that it required four men to raise it whenever he wanted to exert the power of his venomed glance over his enemies. He was slain at last in single combat, according to the ancient legend, at the great battle of Magh-Tura (the plain of the towers), fought between the

Firbolgs and the Tuatha-de-Dananns for the possession of
Ireland several centuries before the Christian era; for before
Balor's brow could be lifted so that he could transfix his enemy
and strike him dead with the terrible power of his glance, his
adversary flung a stone with such violence that it went right
through the Evil Eye, and pierced the skull, and the mighty
magician fell to rise no more.

An interesting account of this battle, with a remarkable
confirmation of the legends respecting it still current in the
district, is given by Sir William Wilde, in his work, "Lough
Corrib; its Shores and Islands." In the ancient manuscript, it
is recorded that a young hero having been slain while bravely
defending his king, the Firbolg army erected a mound over
him, each man carrying a stone, and the monument was
henceforth known as the Carn-in-en-Fhir (the cairn of the one
man). Having examined the locality with a transcript of this
manuscript in his hand, Sir William fixed on the particular
mound, amongst the many stone tumuli scattered over the
plain, which seemed to agree best with the description, and
had it opened carefully under his own superintendence.

A large flag-stone was first discovered, laid
horizontally; then another beneath it, covering a small square
chamber formed of stones, within which was a single urn of
baked clay, graceful and delicate in form and ornamentation,
containing incinerated human bones, the remains, there can be
no reason to doubt, of the Firbolg youth who was honoured for
his loyalty by the erection over him of the Carn-in-en-Fhir on
the historic plains of Mayo.

After Balor, the only other ancient instance of the fatal
effects of the malific Eye is narrated of St. Silan, who had a
poisonous hair in his eyebrow that killed whoever looked first
on him in the morning. All persons, therefore, who from long
sickness, or sorrow, or the weariness that comes with years,
were tired of life, used to try and come in the saint's way, that
so their sufferings might be ended by a quick and easy death.
But another saint, the holy Molaise, hearing that St. Silan
was coming to visit his church, resolved that no more deaths

should happen by means of the poisoned hair. So he arose early in the morning, before anyone was up, and went forth alone to meet St. Silan, and when he saw him coming along the path, he went boldly up and plucked out the fatal hair from his eyebrow, but in doing so he himself was struck by the venom, and immediately after fell down dead.

The power of the Evil Eye was recognized by the Brehon laws, and severe measures were ordained against the users of the malign influence. "If a person is in the habit of injuring things through neglect, or of will, whether he has blessed, or whether he has not blessed, full penalty be upon him, or restitution in kind." So ran the ancient law.

The gift comes by nature and is born with one, though it may not be called into exercise unless circumstances arise to excite the power. Then it seems to act like a spirit of bitter and malicious envy that radiates a poisonous atmosphere which chills and blights everything within its reach. Without being superstitious everyone has felt that there is such a power and succumbed to its influence in a helpless, passive way, as if all self-trust and self-reliant energy were utterly paralyzed by its influence.

Suspected persons are held in great dread by the peasantry, and they recognize them at once by certain signs. Men and women with dark lowering eyebrows are especially feared, and the handsome children are kept out of their path lest they might be overlooked by them.

Red hair is supposed to have a most malign influence, and it has even passed into a proverb: "Let not the eye of a red-haired woman rest on you."

Many persons are quite unconscious that their glance or frown has this evil power until some calamity results, and then they strive not to look at any one full in the face, but to avert their eyes when speaking, lest misfortune might fall upon the person addressed.

The saving invocation, "God bless it!" is universally used when praise is bestowed, to prevent danger, and should a child fall sick someone is immediately suspected of having omitted the usual phrase out of malice and ill-will. Nothing is more dreaded by the peasantry than the full, fixed, direct glance of one suspected of the Evil Eye, and should it fall upon them, or on any of their household, a terrible fear and trembling of heart takes possession of them, which often ends in sickness or sometimes even in death. Some years ago a woman living in Kerry declared that she was "overlooked" by the Evil Eye. She had no pleasure in her life and no comfort, and she wasted away because of the fear that was on her, caused by the following singular circumstance:—

Every time that she happened to leave home alone, and that no one was within call, she was met by a woman totally unknown to her, who, fixing her eyes on her in silence, with a terrible expression, cast her to the ground and proceeded to beat and pinch her till she was nearly senseless; after which her tormentor disappeared.

Having experienced this treatment several times, the poor woman finally abstained altogether from leaving the house, unless protected by a servant or companion; and this precaution she observed for several years, during which time she never was molested. So at last she began to believe that the spell was broken, and that her strange enemy had departed for ever.

In consequence she grew less careful about the usual precaution, and one day stepped down alone to a little stream that ran by the house to wash some clothes.

Stooping down over her work, she never thought of any danger, and began to sing as she used to do in the light-hearted days before the spell was on her, when suddenly a dark shadow fell across the water, and looking up, she beheld to her horror the strange woman on the opposite side of the little stream, with her terrible eyes intently fixed on her, as hard and still as if she were of stone.

Springing up with a scream of terror, she flung down her work, and ran towards the house; but soon she heard footsteps behind her, and in an instant she was seized, thrown down to the ground, and her tormentor began to beat her even worse than before, till she lost all consciousness; and in this state she was found by her husband, lying on her face and speechless. She was at once carried to the house, and all the care that affection and rural skill could bestow were lavished on her, but in vain. She, however, regained sufficient consciousness to tell them of the terrible encounter she had gone through, but died before the night had passed away.

It was believed that the power of fascination by the glance, which is not necessarily an evil power like the Evil Eye, was possessed in a remarkable degree by learned and wise people, especially poets, so that they could make themselves loved and followed by any girl they liked, simply by the influence of the glance. About the year 1790, a young man resided in the County Limerick, who had this power in a singular and unusual degree. He was a clever, witty rhymer in the Irish language; and, probably, had the deep poet eyes that characterize warm and passionate poet natures—eyes that even without necromancy have been known to exercise a powerful magnetic influence over female minds.

One day, while travelling far from home, he came upon a bright, pleasant-looking farmhouse, and feeling weary, he stopped and requested a drink of milk and leave to rest. The farmer's daughter, a young, handsome girl, not liking to admit a stranger, as all the maids were churning, and she was alone in the house, refused him admittance.

The young poet fixed his eyes earnestly on her face for some time in silence, then slowly turning round left the house, and walked towards a small grove of trees just opposite. There he stood for a few moments resting against a tree, and facing the house as if to take one last vengeful or admiring glance, then went his way without once turning round.

The young girl had been watching him from the windows, and the moment he moved she passed out, of the door like one in a dream, and followed him slowly, step by step, down the avenue. The maids grew alarmed, and called to her father, who ran out and shouted loudly for her to stop, but she never turned or seemed to heed. The young man, however, looked round, and seeing the whole family in pursuit, quickened his pace, first glancing fixedly at the girl for a moment. Immediately she sprang towards him, and they were both almost out of sight, when one of the maids espied a piece of paper tied to a branch of the tree where the poet had rested. From curiosity she took it down, and the moment the knot was untied, the farmer's daughter suddenly stopped, became quite still, and when her father came up she allowed him to lead her back to the house without resistance.

When questioned, she said that she felt herself drawn by an invisible force to follow the young stranger wherever he might lead, and that she would have followed him through the world, for her life seemed to be bound up in his; she had no will to resist, and was conscious of nothing else but his presence. Suddenly, however, the spell was broken, and then she heard her father's voice, and knew how strangely she had acted. At the same time the power of the young man over her vanished, and the impulse to follow him was no longer in her heart.

The paper, on being opened, was found to contain five mysterious words written in blood, and in this order—

Sator.
Arepo.
Tenet.
Opera.
Rotas.

These letters are so arranged that read in any way, right to left, left to right, up or down, the same words are produced; and when written in blood with a pen made of an eagle's feather, they form a charm which no woman (it is said) can resist; but the incredulous reader can easily test the truth of this assertion for himself.

Frankenstein Excerpt

Mary Shelley

It was on a dreary night of November that I beheld the accomplishment of my toils. With an anxiety that almost amounted to agony, I collected the instruments of life around me, that I might infuse a spark of being into the lifeless thing that lay at my feet. It was already one in the morning; the rain pattered dismally against the panes, and my candle was nearly burnt out, when, by the glimmer of the half-extinguished light, I saw the dull yellow eye of the creature open; it breathed hard, and a convulsive motion agitated its limbs.

How can I describe my emotions at this catastrophe, or how delineate the wretch whom with such infinite pains and care I had endeavoured to form? His limbs were in proportion, and I had selected his features as beautiful. Beautiful! Great God! His yellow skin scarcely covered the work of muscles and arteries beneath; his hair was of a lustrous black, and flowing; his teeth of a pearly whiteness; but these luxuriances only formed a more horrid contrast with his watery eyes, that seemed almost of the same colour as the dun white sockets in which they were set, his shrivelled complexion and straight black lips.

The different accidents of life are not so changeable as the feelings of human nature. I had worked hard for nearly two years, for the sole purpose of infusing life into an inanimate body. For this I had deprived myself of rest and health. I had desired it with an ardour that far exceeded moderation; but now that I had finished, the beauty of the dream vanished, and breathless horror and disgust filled my heart. Unable to endure the aspect of the being I had created, I rushed out of the room, and continued a long time traversing my bedchamber, unable to compose my mind to sleep. At length lassitude succeeded to the tumult I had before endured; and I threw myself on the bed in my clothes, endeavouring to seek a few moments of forgetfulness. But it was in vain: I slept, indeed, but I was disturbed by the wildest dreams. I thought I saw Elizabeth, in the bloom of health, walking in the streets of Ingolstadt. Delighted and surprised, I embraced her; but as I imprinted the first kiss on her lips, they became livid with the hue of death; her features appeared to change, and I thought that I held the corpse of my dead mother in my arms; a shroud enveloped her form, and I saw the grave-worms crawling in the folds of the flannel. I started from my sleep with horror; a cold dew covered my forehead, my teeth chattered, and every limb became convulsed: when, by the dim and yellow light of the moon, as it forced its way through the window shutters, I beheld the wretch — the miserable monster whom I had created. He held up the curtain of the bed; and his eyes, if eyes they may be called, were fixed on me. His jaws opened, and he muttered some inarticulate sounds, while a grin wrinkled his cheeks. He might have spoken, but I did not hear; one hand was stretched out, seemingly to detain me, but I escaped, and rushed down stairs. I took refuge in the courtyard belonging to the house which I inhabited; where I remained during the rest of the night, walking up and down in the greatest agitation, listening attentively, catching and fearing each sound as if it were to announce the approach of the demoniacal corpse to which I had so miserably given life.

Oh! no mortal could support the horror of that countenance. A mummy again endued with animation could not be so hideous as that wretch. I had gazed on him while unfinished; he was ugly then; but when those muscles and joints were rendered capable of motion, it became a thing such as even Dante could not have conceived.

I passed the night wretchedly. Sometimes my pulse beat so quickly and hardly that I felt the palpitation of every artery; at others, I nearly sank to the ground through languor and extreme weakness. Mingled with this horror, I felt the bitterness of disappointment; dreams that had been my food and pleasant rest for so long a space were now become a hell to me; and the change was so rapid, the overthrow so complete!

Morning, dismal and wet, at length dawned, and discovered to my sleepless and aching eyes the church of Ingolstadt, its white steeple and clock, which indicated the sixth hour. The porter opened the gates of the court, which had that night been my asylum, and I issued into the streets, pacing them with quick steps, as if I sought to avoid the wretch whom I feared every turning of the street would present to my view. I did not dare return to the apartment which I inhabited, but felt impelled to hurry on, although drenched by the rain which poured from a black and comfortless sky.

I continued walking in this manner for some time, endeavouring, by bodily exercise, to ease the load that weighed upon my mind. I traversed the streets, without any clear conception of where I was, or what I was doing. My heart palpitated in the sickness of fear; and I hurried on with irregular steps, not daring to look about me:

"Like one who, on a lonely road, Doth walk in fear and dread, And, having once turned round, walks on, And turns no more his head; Because he knows a frightful fiend Doth close behind him tread."

Coleridge's Ancient Mariner.

Continuing thus, I came at length opposite to the inn at which the various diligences and carriages usually stopped. Here I paused, I knew not why; but I remained some minutes with my eyes fixed on a coach that was coming towards me from the other end of the street. As it drew nearer, I observed that it was the Swiss diligence: it stopped just where I was standing, and, on the door being opened, I perceived Henry Clerval, who, on seeing me, instantly sprung out. "My dear Frankenstein," exclaimed he, "how glad I am to see you! how fortunate that you should be here at the very moment of my alighting!"

Nothing could equal my delight on seeing Clerval; his presence brought back to my thoughts my father, Elizabeth, and all those scenes of home so dear to my recollection. I grasped his hand, and in a moment forgot my horror and misfortune; I felt suddenly, and for the first time during many months, calm and serene joy. I welcomed my friend, therefore, in the most cordial manner, and we walked towards my college. Clerval continued talking for some time about our mutual friends, and his own good fortune in being permitted to come to Ingolstadt. "You may easily believe," said he, "how great was the difficulty to persuade my father that all necessary knowledge was not comprised in the noble art of bookkeeping; and, indeed, I believe I left him incredulous to the last, for his constant answer to my unwearied entreaties was the same as that of the Dutch schoolmaster in the Vicar of Wakefield 'I have ten thousand florins a year without Greek, I eat heartily without Greek.' But his affection for me at length overcame his dislike of learning, and he has permitted me to undertake a voyage of discovery to the land of knowledge."

"It gives me the greatest delight to see you; but tell me how you left my father, brothers, and Elizabeth."

"Very well, and very happy, only a little uneasy that they hear from you so seldom. By the by, I mean to lecture you a little upon their account myself. But, my dear Frankenstein," continued he, stopping short, and gazing full in my face, "I did not before remark how very ill you appear; so thin and pale; you look as if you had been watching for several nights."

"You have guessed right; I have lately been so deeply engaged in one occupation that I have not allowed myself sufficient rest, as you see: but I hope, I sincerely hope, that all these employments are now at an end, and that I am at length free."

I trembled excessively; I could not endure to think of, and far less to allude to, the occurrences of the preceding night. I walked with a quick pace, and we soon arrived at my college. I then reflected, and the thought made me shiver, that the creature whom I had left in my apartment might still be there, alive, and walking about. I dreaded to behold this monster; but I feared still more that Henry should see him. Entreating him, therefore, to remain a few minutes at the bottom of the stairs, I darted up towards my own room. My hand was already on the lock of the door before I recollected myself. I then paused; and a cold shivering came over me. I threw the door forcibly open, as children are accustomed to do when they expect a spectre to stand in waiting for them on the other side; but nothing appeared. I stepped fearfully in: the apartment was empty; and my bedroom was also freed from its hideous guest. I could hardly believe that so great a good fortune could have befallen me; but when I became assured that my enemy had indeed fled, I clapped my hands for joy, and ran down to Clerval.

We ascended into my room, and the servant presently brought breakfast; but I was unable to contain myself. It was not joy only that possessed me; I felt my flesh tingle with excess of sensitiveness, and my pulse beat rapidly. I was unable to remain for a single instant in the same place; I jumped over the chairs, clapped my hands, and laughed aloud. Clerval at first attributed my unusual spirits to joy on his arrival; but when he observed me more attentively he saw a wildness in my eyes for which he could not account; and my loud, unrestrained, heartless laughter, frightened and astonished him.

"My dear Victor," cried he, "what, for God's sake, is the matter? Do not laugh in that manner. How ill you are! What is the cause of all this?"

"Do not ask me," cried I, putting my hands before my eyes, for I thought I saw the dreaded spectre glide into the room; " he can tell. Oh, save me! save me!" I imagined that the monster seized me; I struggled furiously, and fell down in a fit. Poor Clerval!

What must have been his feelings? A meeting, which he anticipated with such joy, so strangely turned to bitterness. But I was not the witness of his grief; for I was lifeless, and did not recover my senses for a long, long time.

This was the commencement of a nervous fever, which confined me for several months. During all that time Henry was my only nurse. I afterwards learned that, knowing my father's advanced age, and unfitness for so long a journey, and how wretched my sickness would make Elizabeth, he spared them this grief by concealing the extent of my disorder. He knew that I could not have a more kind and attentive nurse than himself; and, firm in the hope he felt of my recovery, he did not doubt that, instead of doing harm, he performed the kindest action that he could towards them.

But I was in reality very ill; and surely nothing but the unbounded and unremitting attentions of my friend could have restored me to life. The form of the monster on whom I had bestowed existence was for ever before my eyes, and I raved incessantly concerning him. Doubtless my words surprised Henry: he at first believed them to be the wanderings of my disturbed imagination; but the pertinacity with which I continually recurred to the same subject, persuaded him that my disorder indeed owed its origin to some uncommon and terrible event.

By very slow degrees, and with frequent relapses that alarmed and grieved my friend, I recovered. I remember the first time I became capable of observing outward objects with any kind of pleasure, I perceived that the fallen leaves had disappeared, and that the young buds were shooting forth from the trees that shaded my window. It was a divine spring; and the season contributed greatly to my convalescence. I felt also sentiments of joy and affection revive in my bosom; my gloom disappeared, and in a short time I became as cheerful as before I was attacked by the fatal passion.

"Dearest Clerval," exclaimed I, "how kind, how very good you are to me. This whole winter, instead of being spent in study, as you promised yourself, has been consumed in my sick room. How shall I ever repay you? I feel the greatest remorse for the disappointment of which I have been the occasion; but you will forgive me."

"You will repay me entirely, if you do not discompose yourself, but get well as fast as you can; and since you appear in such good spirits, I may speak to you on one subject, may I not?"

I trembled. One subject! What could it be? Could he allude to an object on whom I dared not even think?

"Compose yourself," said Clerval, who observed my change of colour, "I will not mention it, if it agitates you; but your father and cousin would be very happy if they received a letter from you in your own handwriting. They hardly know how ill you have been, and are uneasy at your long silence."

"Is that all, my dear Henry? How could you suppose that my first thoughts would not fly towards those dear, dear friends whom I love, and who are so deserving of my love."

"If this is your present temper, my friend, you will perhaps be glad to see a letter that has been lying here some days for you; it is from your cousin, I believe."

Man-Size in Marble

Edith Nesbit

Although every word of this story is as true as despair, I do not expect people to believe it. Nowadays a "rational explanation" is required before belief is possible. Let me then, at once, offer the "rational explanation" which finds most favour among those who have heard the tale of my life's tragedy. It is held that we were "under a delusion," Laura and I, on that 31st of October; and that this supposition places the whole matter on a satisfactory and believable basis. The reader can judge, when he, too, has heard my story, how far this is an "explanation," and in what sense it is "rational." There were three who took part in this: Laura and I and another man. The other man still lives, and can speak to the truth of the least credible part of my story.

I never in my life knew what it was to have as much money as I required to supply the most ordinary needs—good colours, books, and cab-fares—and when we were married we knew quite well that we should only be able to live at all by "strict punctuality and attention to business." I used to paint in those days, and Laura used to write, and we felt sure we could keep the pot at least simmering. Living in town was out of the question, so we went to look for a cottage in the country, which should be at once sanitary and picturesque. So rarely do these two qualities meet in one cottage that our search was for some time quite fruitless. We tried advertisements, but most of the desirable rural residences which we did look at proved to be lacking in both essentials, and when a cottage chanced to have drains it always had stucco as well and was shaped like a tea-caddy. And if we found a vine or rose-covered porch, corruption invariably lurked within. Our minds got so befogged by the eloquence of house-agents and the rival disadvantages of the fever-traps and outrages to beauty which we had seen and scorned, that I very much doubt whether either of us, on our wedding morning, knew the difference between a house and a haystack. But when we got away from friends and house-agents, on our honeymoon, our wits grew clear again, and we knew a pretty cottage when at last we saw one. It was at Brenzett—a little village set on a hill over against the southern marshes. We had gone there, from the seaside village where we were staying, to see the church, and two fields from the church we found this cottage. It stood quite by itself, about two miles from the village. It was a long, low building, with rooms sticking out in unexpected places. There was a bit of stone-work—ivy-covered and moss-grown, just two old rooms, all that was left of a big house that had once stood there—and round this stone-work the house had grown up.

Stripped of its roses and jasmine it would have been hideous. As it stood it was charming, and after a brief examination we took it. It was absurdly cheap. The rest of our honeymoon we spent in grubbing about in second-hand shops in the county town, picking up bits of old oak and Chippendale chairs for our furnishing. We wound up with a run up to town and a visit to Liberty's, and soon the low oak-beamed lattice-windowed rooms began to be home. There was a jolly old-fashioned garden, with grass paths, and no end of hollyhocks and sunflowers, and big lilies. From the window you could see the marsh-pastures, and beyond them the blue, thin line of the sea. We were as happy as the summer was glorious, and settled down into work sooner than we ourselves expected. I was never tired of sketching the view and the wonderful cloud effects from the open lattice, and Laura would sit at the table and write verses about them, in which I mostly played the part of foreground.

We got a tall old peasant woman to do for us. Her face and figure were good, though her cooking was of the homeliest; but she understood all about gardening, and told us all the old names of the coppices and cornfields, and the stories of the smugglers and highwaymen, and, better still, of the "things that walked," and of the "sights" which met one in lonely glens of a starlight night. She was a great comfort to us, because Laura hated housekeeping as much as I loved folklore, and we soon came to leave all the domestic business to Mrs. Dorman, and to use her legends in little magazine stories which brought in the jingling guinea.

We had three months of married happiness, and did not have a single quarrel. One October evening I had been down to smoke a pipe with the doctor—our only neighbour—a pleasant young Irishman. Laura had stayed at home to finish a comic sketch of a village episode for the Monthly Marplot. I left her laughing over her own jokes, and came in to find her a crumpled heap of pale muslin weeping on the window seat. "Good heavens, my darling, what's the matter?" I cried, taking her in my arms. She leaned her little dark head against my shoulder and went on crying. I had never seen her cry before—we had always been so happy, you see—and I felt sure some frightful misfortune had happened.

"What is the matter? Do speak."

"It's Mrs. Dorman," she sobbed.

"What has she done?" I inquired, immensely relieved.

"She says she must go before the end of the month, and she says her niece is ill; she's gone down to see her now, but I don't believe that's the reason, because her niece is always ill. I believe someone has been setting her against us. Her manner was so queer....."

"Never mind, Pussy," I said; "whatever you do, don't cry, or I shall have to cry too, to keep you in countenance, and then you'll never respect your man again!"

She dried her eyes obediently on my handkerchief, and even smiled faintly.

"But you see," she went on, "it is really serious, because these village people are so sheepy, and if one won't do a thing you may be quite sure none of the others will. And I shall have to cook the dinners, and wash up the hateful greasy plates; and you'll have to carry cans of water about, and clean the boots and knives—and we shall never have any time for work, or earn any money, or anything. We shall have to work all day, and only be able to rest when we are waiting for the kettle to boil!"

I represented to her that even if we had to perform these duties, the day would still present some margin for other toils and recreations. But she refused to see the matter in any but the greyest light. She was very unreasonable, my Laura, but I could not have loved her any more if she had been as reasonable as Whately.

"I'll speak to Mrs. Dorman when she comes back, and see if I can't come to terms with her," I said. "Perhaps she wants a rise in her screw. It will be all right. Let's walk up to the church."

The church was a large and lonely one, and we loved to go there, especially upon bright nights. The path skirted a wood, cut through it once, and ran along the crest of the hill through two meadows, and round the churchyard wall, over which the old yews loomed in black masses of shadow. This path, which was partly paved, was called "the bier-balk," for it had long been the way by which the corpses had been carried to burial. The churchyard was richly treed, and was shaded by great elms which stood just outside and stretched their majestic arms in benediction over the happy dead. A large, low porch let one into the building by a Norman doorway and a heavy oak door studded with iron. Inside, the arches rose into darkness, and between them the reticulated windows, which stood out white in the moonlight. In the chancel, the windows were of rich glass, which showed in faint light their noble colouring, and made the black oak of the choir pews hardly more solid than the shadows. But on each side of the altar lay a grey marble figure of a knight in full plate armour lying upon a low slab, with hands held up in everlasting prayer, and these figures, oddly enough, were always to be seen if there was any glimmer of light in the church. Their names were lost, but the peasants told of them that they had been fierce and wicked men, marauders by land and sea, who had been the scourge of their time, and had been guilty of deeds so foul that the house they had lived in—the big house, by the way, that had stood on the site of our cottage—had been stricken by lightning and the vengeance of Heaven. But for all that, the gold of their heirs had bought them a place in the church. Looking at the bad hard faces reproduced in the marble, this story was easily believed.

The church looked at its best and weirdest on that night, for the shadows of the yew trees fell through the windows upon the floor of the nave and touched the pillars with tattered shade. We sat down together without speaking, and watched the solemn beauty of the old church, with some of that awe which inspired its early builders. We walked to the chancel and looked at the sleeping warriors. Then we rested some time on the stone seat in the porch, looking out over the stretch of quiet moonlit meadows, feeling in every fibre of our being the peace of the night and of our happy love; and came away at last with a sense that even scrubbing and blackleading were but small troubles at their worst.

Mrs. Dorman had come back from the village, and I at once invited her to a tête-à-tête. "Now, Mrs. Dorman," I said, when I had got her into my painting room, "what's all this about your not staying with us?"

"I should be glad to get away, sir, before the end of the month," she answered, with her usual placid dignity.

"Have you any fault to find, Mrs. Dorman?"

"None at all, sir; you and your lady have always been most kind, I'm sure——"

"Well, what is it? Are your wages not high enough?"

"No, sir, I gets quite enough."

"Then why not stay?"

"I'd rather not"—with some hesitation—"my niece is ill."

"But your niece has been ill ever since we came."

No answer. There was a long and awkward silence. I broke it.

"Can't you stay for another month?" I asked.

"No, sir. I'm bound to go by Thursday."

And this was Monday!

"Well, I must say, I think you might have let us know

before. There's no time now to get any one else, and your mistress is not fit to do heavy housework. Can't you stay till next week?"

"I might be able to come back next week."

I was now convinced that all she wanted was a brief holiday, which we should have been willing enough to let her have, as soon as we could get a substitute.

"But why must you go this week?" I persisted. "Come, out with it."

Mrs. Dorman drew the little shawl, which she always wore, tightly across her bosom, as though she were cold. Then she said, with a sort of effort—

"They say, sir, as this was a big house in Catholic times, and there was a many deeds done here."

The nature of the "deeds" might be vaguely inferred from the inflection of Mrs. Dorman's voice—which was enough to make one's blood run cold. I was glad that Laura was not in the room.   She was always nervous, as highly-strung natures are, and I felt that these tales about our house, told by this old peasant woman, with her impressive manner and contagious credulity, might have made our home less dear to my wife.

"Tell me all about it, Mrs. Dorman," I said; "you needn't mind about telling me. I'm not like the young people who make fun of such things."

Which was partly true.

"Well, sir"—she sank her voice—"you may have seen in the church, beside the altar, two shapes."

"You mean the effigies of the knights in armour," I said cheerfully.

"I mean them two bodies, drawed out man-size in marble," she returned, and I had to admit that her description was a thousand times more graphic than mine, to say nothing of a certain weird force and uncanniness about the phrase "drawed out man-size in marble."

"They do say, as on All Saints' Eve them two bodies sits up on their slabs, and gets off of them, and then walks down the aisle, in their marble"—(another good phrase, Mrs. Dorman)—"and as the church clock strikes eleven they walks out of the church door, and over the graves, and along the bier-balk, and if it's a wet night there's the marks of their feet in the morning."

"And where do they go?" I asked, rather fascinated.

"They comes back here to their home, sir, and if any one meets them—"

"Well, what then?" I asked.

But no—not another word could I get from her, save that her niece was ill and she must go. After what I had heard I scorned to discuss the niece, and tried to get from Mrs. Dorman more details of the legend. I could get nothing but warnings.

"Whatever you do, sir, lock the door early on All Saints' Eve, and make the cross-sign over the doorstep and on the windows."

"But has any one ever seen these things?" I persisted.

"That's not for me to say. I know what I know, sir."

"Well, who was here last year?"

"No one, sir; the lady as owned the house only stayed here in summer, and she always went to London a full month afore the night. And I'm sorry to inconvenience you and your lady, but my niece is ill and I must go on Thursday."

I could have shaken her for her absurd reiteration of that obvious fiction, after she had told me her real reasons. She was determined to go, nor could our united entreaties move her in the least.

I did not tell Laura the legend of the shapes that "walked in their marble," partly because a legend concerning our house might perhaps trouble my wife, and partly, I think, from some more occult reason. This was not quite the same to me as any other story, and I did not want to talk about it till the day was over. I had very soon ceased to think of the legend, however. I was painting a portrait of Laura, against the lattice window, and I could not think of much else. I had got a splendid background of yellow and grey sunset, and was working away with enthusiasm at her face. On Thursday Mrs. Dorman went. She relented, at parting, so far as to say—

"Don't you put yourself about too much, ma'am, and if there's any little thing I can do next week, I'm sure I shan't mind." From which I inferred that she wished to come back to us after Halloween. Up to the last she adhered to the fiction of the niece with touching fidelity.

Thursday passed off pretty well. Laura showed marked ability in the matter of steak and potatoes, and I confess that my knives, and the plates, which I insisted upon washing, were better done than I had dared to expect.

Friday came. It is about what happened on that Friday that this is written. I wonder if I should have believed it, if anyone had told it to me. I will write the story of it as quickly and plainly as I can. Everything that happened on that day is burnt into my brain. I shall not forget anything, nor leave anything out.

I got up early, I remember, and lighted the kitchen fire, and had just achieved a smoky success, when my little wife came running down, as sunny and sweet as the clear October morning itself. We prepared breakfast together, and found it very good fun. The housework was soon done, and when brushes and brooms and pails were quiet again, the house was still indeed. It is wonderful what a difference one makes in a house. We really missed Mrs. Dorman, quite apart from considerations concerning pots and pans. We spent the day in dusting our books and putting them straight, and dined gaily on cold steak and coffee. Laura was, if possible, brighter and gayer and sweeter than usual, and I began to think that a little domestic toil was really good for her. We had never been so merry since we were married, and the walk we had that afternoon was, I think, the happiest time of all my life. When we had watched the deep scarlet clouds slowly pale into leaden grey against a pale-green sky, and saw the white mists curl up along the hedgerows in the distant marsh, we came back to the house, silently, hand in hand.

"You are sad, my darling," I said, half-jestingly, as we sat down together in our little parlour. I expected a disclaimer, for my own silence had been the silence of complete happiness. To my surprise she said—

"Yes. I think I am sad, or rather I am uneasy. I don't think I'm very well. I have shivered three or four times since we came in, and it is not cold, is it?"

"No," I said, and hoped it was not a chill caught from the treacherous mists that roll up from the marshes in the dying light. No—she said, she did not think so. Then, after a silence, she spoke suddenly—

"Do you ever have presentiments of evil?"

"No," I said, smiling, "and I shouldn't believe in them if I had."

"I do," she went on; "the night my father died I knew it, though he was right away in the north of Scotland." I did not answer in words. She sat looking at the fire for some time in silence, gently stroking my hand. At last she sprang up, came behind me, and, drawing my head back, kissed me.

"There, it's over now," she said. "What a baby I am! Come, light the candles, and we'll have some of these new Rubinstein duets."

And we spent a happy hour or two at the piano.

At about half-past ten I began to long for the good-night pipe, but Laura looked so white that I felt it would be brutal of me to fill our sitting-room with the fumes of strong cavendish.

"I'll take my pipe outside," I said.

"Let me come, too."

"No, sweetheart, not to-night; you're much too tired. I shan't be long. Get to bed, or I shall have an invalid to nurse tomorrow as well as the boots to clean."

I kissed her and was turning to go, when she flung her arms round my neck, and held me as if she would never let me go again. I stroked her hair.

"Come, Pussy, you're over-tired. The housework has been too much for you."

She loosened her clasp a little and drew a deep breath.

"No. We've been very happy today, Jack, haven't we? Don't stay out too long."

"I won't, my dearie."

I strolled out of the front door, leaving it unlatched. What a night it was! The jagged masses of heavy dark cloud were rolling at intervals from horizon to horizon, and thin white wreaths covered the stars. Through all the rush of the cloud river, the moon swam, breasting the waves and disappearing again in the darkness. When now and again her light reached the woodlands they seemed to be slowly and noiselessly waving in time to the swing of the clouds above them. There was a strange grey light over all the earth; the fields had that shadowy bloom over them which only comes from the marriage of dew and moonshine, or frost and starlight.

I walked up and down, drinking in the beauty of the quiet earth and the changing sky. The night was absolutely silent. Nothing seemed to be abroad. There was no skurrying of rabbits, or twitter of the half-asleep birds. And though the clouds went sailing across the sky, the wind that drove them never came low enough to rustle the dead leaves in the woodland paths. Across the meadows I could see the church tower standing out black and grey against the sky. I walked there thinking over our three months of happiness—and of my wife, her dear eyes, her loving ways. Oh, my little girl! my own little girl; what a vision came then of a long, glad life for you and me together!

I heard a bell-beat from the church. Eleven already! I turned to go in, but the night held me. I could not go back into our little warm rooms yet. I would go up to the church. I felt vaguely that it would be good to carry my love and thankfulness to the sanctuary whither so many loads of sorrow and gladness had been borne by the men and women of the dead years.

I looked in at the low window as I went by. Laura was half lying on her chair in front of the fire. I could not see her face, only her little head showed dark against the pale blue wall. She was quite still. Asleep, no doubt. My heart reached out to her, as I went on. There must be a God, I thought, and a God who was good. How otherwise could anything so sweet and dear as she have ever been imagined?

I walked slowly along the edge of the wood. A sound broke the stillness of the night, it was a rustling in the wood. I stopped and listened. The sound stopped too. I went on, and now distinctly heard another step than mine answer mine like an echo. It was a poacher or a wood-stealer, most likely, for these were not unknown in our Arcadian neighbourhood. But whoever it was, he was a fool not to step more lightly. I turned into the wood, and now the footstep seemed to come from the path I had just left. It must be an echo, I thought. The wood looked perfect in the moonlight The large dying ferns and the brushwood showed where through thinning foliage the pale light came down. The tree trunks stood up like Gothic columns all around me. They reminded me of the church, and I turned into the bier-balk, and passed through the corpse-gate between the graves to the low porch. I paused for a moment on the stone seat where Laura and I had watched the fading landscape. Then I noticed that the door of the church was open, and I blamed myself for having left it unlatched the other night. We were the only people who ever cared to come to the church except on Sundays, and I was vexed to think that through our carelessness the damp autumn airs had had a chance of getting in and injuring the old fabric. I went in. It will seem strange, perhaps, that I should have gone half-way up the aisle before I remembered—with a sudden chill, followed by as sudden a rush of self-contempt—that this was the very day and hour when, according to tradition, the "shapes drawed out, man-size in marble" began to walk.

Having thus remembered the legend, and remembered it with a shiver, of which I was ashamed, I could not do otherwise than walk up towards the altar, just to look at the figures—as I said to myself; really what I wanted was to assure myself, first, that I did not believe the legend, and, secondly, that it was not true. I was rather glad that I had come. I thought now I could tell Mrs. Dorman how vain her fancies were, and how peacefully the marble figures slept on through the ghastly hour. With my hands in my pockets I passed up the aisle. In the grey dim light the eastern end of the church looked larger than usual, and the arches above the two tombs looked larger too. The moon came out and showed me the reason. I stopped short, my heart gave a leap that nearly choked me, and then sank sickeningly. The "bodies drawed out, man-size" were gone, and their marble slabs lay wide and bare in the vague moonlight that slanted through the east window.

Were they really gone? or was I mad? Clenching my nerves, I stooped and passed my hand over the smooth slabs, and felt their flat unbroken surface. Had someone taken the things away? Was it some vile practical joke? I would make sure, anyway. In an instant I had made a torch of a newspaper, which happened to be in my pocket, and lighting it held it high above my head. Its yellow glare illumined the dark arches and those slabs. The figures were gone.

And I was alone in the church; or was I alone? And then a horror seized me, a horror indefinable and indescribable—an overwhelming certainty of supreme and accomplished calamity. I flung down the torch and tore along the aisle and out through the porch, biting my lips as I ran to keep myself from shrieking aloud. Oh, was I mad—or what was this that possessed me? I leaped the churchyard wall and took the straight cut across the fields, led by the light from our windows. Just as I got over the first stile, a dark figure seemed to spring out of the ground. Mad still with that certainty of misfortune, I made for the thing that stood in my path, shouting, "Get out of the way, can't you!"

But my push met with a more vigorous resistance than I had expected. My arms were caught just above the elbow and held as in a vice, and the raw-boned Irish doctor actually shook me.

"Would ye?" he cried, in his own unmistakable accents—"would ye, then?"

"Let me go, you fool," I gasped. "The marble figures

have gone from the church; I tell you they've gone."

He broke into a ringing laugh. "I'll have to give ye a draught to-morrow, I see. Ye've bin smoking too much and listening to old wives' tales."

"I tell you, I've seen the bare slabs."

"Well, come back with me. I'm going up to old Palmer's—his daughter's ill; we'll look in at the church and let me see the bare slabs."

"You go, if you like," I said, a little less frantic for his laughter; "I'm going home to my wife."

"Rubbish, man," said he; "d'ye think I'll permit of that? Are ye to go saying all yer life that ye've seen solid marble endowed with vitality, and me to go all me life saying ye were a coward? No, sir—ye shan't do ut."

The night air—a human voice—and I think also the physical contact with this six feet of solid common sense, brought me back a little to my ordinary self, and the word "coward" was a mental shower-bath.

"Come on, then," I said sullenly; "perhaps you're right."

He still held my arm tightly. We got over the stile and back to the church. All was still as death. The place smelt very damp and earthy. We walked up the aisle. I am not ashamed to confess that I shut my eyes: I knew the figures would not be there. I heard Kelly strike a match.

"Here they are, ye see, right enough; ye've been dreaming or drinking, asking yer pardon for the imputation." I opened my eyes. By Kelly's expiring vesta I saw two shapes lying "in their marble" on their slabs. I drew a deep breath, and caught his hand.

"I'm awfully indebted to you," I said. "It must have been some trick of light, or I have been working rather hard, perhaps that's it. Do you know, I was quite convinced they were gone."

"I'm aware of that," he answered rather grimly; "ye'll have to be careful of that brain of yours, my friend, I assure ye." He was leaning over and looking at the right-hand figure, whose stony face was the most villainous and deadly in expression.

"By Jove," he said, "something has been afoot here—this hand is broken."

And so it was. I was certain that it had been perfect the last time Laura and I had been there.

"Perhaps someone has tried to remove them," said the young doctor.

"That won't account for my impression," I objected.

"Too much painting and tobacco will account for that, well enough."

"Come along," I said, "or my wife will be getting anxious. You'll come in and have a drop of whisky and drink confusion to ghosts and better sense to me."

"I ought to go up to Palmer's, but it's so late now I'd best leave it till the morning," he replied. "I was kept late at the Union, and I've had to see a lot of people since. All right, I'll come back with ye."

I think he fancied I needed him more than did Palmer's girl, so, discussing how such an illusion could have been possible, and deducing from this experience large generalities concerning ghostly apparitions, we walked up to our cottage We saw, as we walked up the garden-path, that bright light streamed out of the front door, and presently saw that the parlour door was open too. Had she gone out?

"Come in," I said, and Dr. Kelly followed me into the parlour. It was all ablaze with candles, not only the wax ones, but at least a dozen guttering, glaring tallow dips, stuck in vases and ornaments in unlikely places. Light, I knew, was Laura's remedy for nervousness. Poor child! Why had I left her? Brute that I was.

We glanced round the room, and at first we did not see her. The window was open, and the draught set all the candles flaring one way. Her chair was empty and her handkerchief and book lay on the floor. I turned to the window. There, in the recess of the window, I saw her. Oh, my child, my love, had she gone to that window to watch for me? And what had come into the room behind her? To what had she turned with that look of frantic fear and horror? Oh, my little one, had she thought that it was I whose step she heard, and turned to meet—what?

She had fallen back across a table in the window, and her body lay half on it and half on the window-seat, and her head hung down over the table, the brown hair loosened and fallen to the carpet. Her lips were drawn back, and her eyes wide, wide open. They saw nothing now. What had they seen last?

The doctor moved towards her, but I pushed him aside and sprang to her; caught her in my arms and cried—
"It's all right, Laura! I've got you safe, wifie."

She fell into my arms in a heap. I clasped her and kissed her, and called her by all her pet names, but I think I knew all the time that she was dead. Her hands were tightly clenched. In one of them she held something fast. When I was quite sure that she was dead, and that nothing mattered at all any more, I let him open her hand to see what she held.

It was a grey marble finger.

Alien Boy

Mary Darby Robinson

'Twas on a Mountain, near the Western Main
An ALIEN dwelt.
A solitary Hut
Built on a jutting crag, o'erhung with weeds,
Mark'd the poor Exile's home.
Full ten long years
The melancholy wretch had liv'd unseen
By all, save HENRY, a lov'd, little Son
The partner of his sorrows.
On the day
When Persecution, in the sainted guise
Of Liberty, spread wide its venom'd pow'r,
The brave, Saint HUBERT, fled his Lordly home,
And, with his baby Son, the mountain sought.

Resolv'd to cherish in his bleeding breast
The secret of his birth, Ah! birth too high
For his now humbled state, from infancy
He taught him, labour's task: He bade him chear
The dreary day of cold adversity
By patience and by toil.
The Summer morn
Shone on the pillow of his rushy bed;
The noontide, sultry hour, he fearless past
On the shagg'd eminence; while the young Kid
Skipp'd, to the cadence of his minstrelsy.

At night young HENRY trimm'd the faggot fire
While oft, Saint HUBERT, wove the ample net
To snare the finny victim.
Oft they sang
And talk'd, while sullenly the waves would sound

Dashing the sandy shore.
Saint HUBERT'S eyes
Would swim in tears of fondness, mix'd with joy,
When he observ'd the op'ning harvest rich
Of promis'd intellect, which HENRY'S soul,
Whate'er the subject of their talk, display'd.

Oft, the bold Youth, in question intricate,
Would seek to know the story of his birth;
Oft ask, who bore him: and with curious skill
Enquire, why he, and only one beside,
Peopled the desart mountain ? Still his Sire
Was slow of answer, and, in words obscure,
Varied the conversation.
Still the mind
Of HENRY ponder'd; for, in their lone hut,
A daily journal would Saint HUBERT make
Of his long banishment: and sometimes speak
Of Friends forsaken, Kindred, massacred;—
Proud mansions, rich domains, and joyous scenes
For ever faded—lost!
One winter time,
'Twas on the Eve of Christmas, the shrill blast
Swept o'er the stormy main.
 The boiling foam
Rose to an altitude so fierce and strong

That their low hovel totter'd.
Oft they stole
To the rock's margin, and with fearful eyes
Mark'd the vex'd deep, as the slow rising moon
Gleam'd on the world of waters.
'Twas a scene
Would make a Stoic shudder! For, amid
The wavy mountains, they beheld, alone ,
A LITTLE BOAT, now scarcely visible;
And now not seen at all; or, like a buoy,

Bounding, and buffetting, to reach the shore!

Now the full Moon, in crimson lustre shone
Upon the outstretch'd Ocean.
The black clouds
Flew stiffly on, the wild blast following,
And, as they flew, dimming the angry main
With shadows horrible ! Still, the small boat
Struggled amid the waves, a sombre speck
Upon the wide domain of howling Death!
Saint HUBERT sigh'd ! while HENRY'S speaking eye
Alternately the stormy scene survey'd
And his low hovel's safety.
So past on
The hour of midnight, and, since first they knew
The solitary scene, no midnight hour
E'er seem'd so long and weary.
While they stood,
Their hands fast link'd together, and their eyes
Fix'd on the troublous Ocean, suddenly
The breakers, bounding on the rocky shore,
Left the small wreck; and crawling on the side
Of the rude crag, a HUMAN FORM was seen!
And now he climb'd the foam-wash'd precipice,
And now the slip'ry weeds gave way, while he
Descended to the sands: The moon rose high—
The wild blast paus'd, and the poor shipwreck'd Man
Look'd round aghast, when on the frowning steep
He marked the lonely exiles.
Now he call'd
But he was feeble, and his voice was lost
Amid the din of mingling sounds that rose
From the wild scene of clamour.
Down the steep
Saint HUBRET hurried, boldly venturous,
Catching the slimy weeds, from point to point,
And unappall'd by peril.

At the foot
Of the rude rock, the fainting mariner
Seiz'd on his outstretch'd arm; impatient, wild,
With transport exquisite ! But ere they heard
The blest exchange of sounds articulate,
A furious billow, rolling on the steep,
Engulph'd them in Oblivion!
On the rock
Young HENRY stood; with palpitating heart,
And fear-struck, e'en to madness ! Now he call'd,
Louder and louder, as the shrill blast blew;
But, mid the elemental strife of sounds,
No human voice gave answer ! The clear moon
No longer quiver'd on the curling main,
But, mist-encircled, shed a blunted light,
Enough to shew all things that mov'd around,
Dreadful, but indistinctly ! The black weeds
Wav'd, as the night-blast swept them; and along
The rocky shore the breakers, sounding low
Seem'd like the whisp'ring of a million souls
Beneath the green-deep mourning.
Four long hours
The lorn Boy listen'd ! four long tedious hours
Pass'd wearily away, when, in the East
The grey beam coldly glimmer'd.
All alone
Young HENRY stood aghast : his Eye wide fix'd;
While his dark locks, uplifted by the storm
Uncover'd met its fury.
On his cheek
Despair sate terrible ! For, mid the woes,
Of poverty and toil, he had not known,
Till then, the horror-giving chearless hour
Of TOTAL SOLITUDE!

He spoke—he groan'd,
But no responsive voice, no kindred tone

Broke the dread pause: For now the storm had ceas'd,
And the bright Sun-beams glitter'd on the breast
Of the green placid Ocean.
To his Hut
The lorn Boy hasten'd; there the rushy couch,
The pillow still indented, met his gaze
And fix'd his eye in madness.
From that hour
A maniac wild, the Alien Boy has been;
His garb with sea-weeds fring'd, and his wan cheek
The tablet of his mind, disorder'd, chang'd,
Fading, and worn with care.
And if, by chance,
A Sea-beat wand'rer from the outstretch'd main
Views the lone Exile, and with gen'rous zeal
Hastes to the sandy beach, he suddenly
Darts 'mid the cavern'd cliffs, and leaves pursuit
To track him, where no footsteps but his own,
Have e'er been known to venture ! YET HE LIVES
A melancholy proof that Man may bear
All the rude storms of Fate, and still suspire
By the wide world forgotten!

Tortured Love

"Love never dies a natural death. It dies because we don't know how to replenish its source. It dies of blindness and errors and betrayals. It dies of illness and wounds; it dies of weariness, of witherings, of tarnishings."
- Anaïs Nin

In the final section, works by Elinor Wylie, Charlotte Perkins-Gilman, Clemence Housman, and Gertrude Atherton are included. These texts all involve various elements of tortured love.

Demon Lovers

Elinor Wylie

The peacock and the mocking-bird
Cry forever in her breast;
Public libraries have blurred
The pages of his palimpsest.
He wanders lonely as a cloud
In chevelure of curled perruque;
Masked assassins in a crowd
Strangle the uxorious duke.
Castilian facing Lucifer,
Juan does not remove his cap;
Unswaddled infantile to her
His soul lies kicking in her lap.
While she, transported by the wind,
Mercutio has clasped and kissed...
Like quicksilver, her absent mind
Evades them both, and is not missed.

The Yellow Wallpaper

Charlotte Perkins Gilman

It is very seldom that mere ordinary people like John and myself secure ancestral halls for the summer.

A colonial mansion, a hereditary estate, I would say a haunted house, and reach the height of romantic felicity—but that would be asking too much of fate!

Still I will proudly declare that there is something queer about it.

Else, why should it be let so cheaply? And why have stood so long untenanted?

John laughs at me, of course, but one expects that in marriage.

John is practical in the extreme. He has no patience with faith, an intense horror of superstition, and he scoffs openly at any talk of things not to be felt and seen and put down in figures.

John is a physician, and perhaps (I would not say it to a living soul, of course, but this is dead paper and a great relief to my mind) perhaps that is one reason I do not get well faster.

You see he does not believe I am sick!

And what can one do?

If a physician of high standing, and one's own husband, assures friends and relatives that there is really nothing the matter with one but temporary nervous depression—a slight hysterical tendency—what is one to do?

My brother is also a physician, and also of high standing, and he says the same thing.

So I take phosphates or phosphites—whichever it is, and tonics, and journeys, and air, and exercise, and am absolutely forbidden to "work" until I am well again.

Personally, I disagree with their ideas.

Personally, I believe that congenial work, with excitement and change, would do me good.

But what is one to do?

I did write for a while in spite of them; but it does exhaust me a good deal—having to be so sly about it, or else meet with heavy opposition.

I sometimes fancy that in my condition if I had less opposition and more society and stimulus—but John says the very worst thing I can do is to think about my condition, and I confess it always makes me feel bad.

So I will let it alone and talk about the house.

The most beautiful place! It is quite alone standing well back from the road, quite three miles from the village. It makes me think of English places that you read about, for there are hedges and walls and gates that lock, and lots of separate little houses for the gardeners and people.

There is a delicious garden! I never saw such a garden-large and shady, full of box-bordered paths, and lined with long grape-covered arbors with seats under them.

There were greenhouses, too, but they are all broken now.

There was some legal trouble, I believe, something about the heirs and coheirs; anyhow, the place has been empty for years.

That spoils my ghostliness, I am afraid, but I don't care—there is something strange about the house—I can feel it.

I even said so to John one moonlight evening but he said what I felt was a draught, and shut the window.

I get unreasonably angry with John sometimes I'm sure I never used to be so sensitive. I think it is due to this nervous condition.

But John says if I feel so, I shall neglect proper self-control; so I take pains to control myself—before him, at least, and that makes me very tired.

I don't like our room a bit. I wanted one downstairs that opened on the piazza and had roses all over the window, and such pretty old-fashioned chintz hangings! But John would not hear of it.

He said there was only one window and not room for

two beds, and no near room for him if he took another.

He is very careful and loving, and hardly lets me stir without special direction.

I have a schedule prescription for each hour in the day; he takes all care from me, and so I feel basely ungrateful not to value it more.

He said we came here solely on my account that I was to have perfect rest and all the air I could get. "Your exercise depends on your strength, my dear," said he, "and your food somewhat on your appetite; but air you can absorb all the time." So we took the nursery at the top of the house.

It is a big, airy room, the whole floor nearly, with windows that look all ways, and air and sunshine galore. It was nursery first and then playroom and gymnasium, I should judge; for the windows are barred for little children, and there are rings and things in the walls.

The paint and paper look as if a boys' school had used it. It is stripped off—the paper in great patches all around the head of my bed, about as far as I can reach, and in a great place on the other side of the room low down. I never saw a worse paper in my life.

One of those sprawling flamboyant patterns committing every artistic sin.

It is dull enough to confuse the eye in following, pronounced enough to constantly irritate and provoke study, and when you follow the lame uncertain curves for a little distance they suddenly commit suicide—plunge off at outrageous angles, destroy themselves in unheard of contradictions.

The color is repellent, almost revolting; a smouldering unclean yellow, strangely faded by the slow-turning sunlight. It is a dull yet lurid orange in some places, a sickly sulphur tint in others.

No wonder the children hated it! I should hate it myself if I had to live in this room long.

There comes John, and I must put this away; he hates to have me write a word.

We have been here two weeks, and I haven't felt like writing before, since that first day.

I am sitting by the window now, up in this atrocious nursery, and there is nothing to hinder my writing as much as I please, save lack of strength.

John is away all day, and even some nights when his cases are serious.

I am glad my case is not serious!

But these nervous troubles are dreadfully depressing.

John does not know how much I really suffer. He knows there is no reason to suffer, and that satisfies him.

Of course it is only nervousness. It does weigh on me so not to do my duty in any way!

I meant to be such a help to John, such a real rest and comfort, and here I am a comparative burden already!

Nobody would believe what an effort it is to do what little I am able; to dress and entertain, and order things.

It is fortunate Mary is so good with the baby. Such a dear baby!

And yet I cannot be with him, it makes me so nervous.

I suppose John never was nervous in his life. He laughs at me so about this wallpaper!

At first he meant to repaper the room, but afterwards he said that I was letting it get the better of me, and that nothing was worse for a nervous patient than to give way to such fancies.

He said that after the wallpaper was changed it would be the heavy bedstead, and then the barred windows, and then that gate at the head of the stairs, and so on.

"You know the place is doing you good," he said, "and really, dear, I don't care to renovate the house just for a three months' rental."

"Then do let us go downstairs," I said, "there are such pretty rooms there."

Then he took me in his arms and called me a blessed little goose, and said he would go down to the cellar, if I wished, and have it whitewashed into the bargain.

But he is right enough about the beds and windows and things.

It is an airy and comfortable room as any one need wish, and, of course, I would not be so silly as to make him uncomfortable just for a whim.

I'm really getting quite fond of the big room, all but that horrid paper.

Out of one window I can see the garden, those mysterious deep shaded arbors, the riotous old-fashioned flowers, and bushes and gnarly trees.

Out of another I get a lovely view of the bay and a little private wharf belonging to the estate. There is a beautiful shaded lane that runs down there from the house. I always fancy I see people walking in these numerous paths and arbors, but John has cautioned me not to give way to fancy in the least. He says that with my imaginative power and habit of story-making, a nervous weakness like mine is sure to lead to all manner of excited fancies, and that I ought to use my will and good sense to check the tendency. So I try.

I think sometimes that if I were only well enough to write a little it would relieve the press of ideas and rest me.

But I find I get pretty tired when I try.

It is so discouraging not to have any advice and companionship about my work. When I get really well, John says we will ask Cousin Henry and Julia down for a long visit; but he says he would as soon put fireworks in my pillow-case as to let me have those stimulating people about now.

I wish I could get well faster.

But I must not think about that. This paper looks to me as if it knew what a vicious influence it had!

There is a recurrent spot where the pattern lolls like a broken neck and two bulbous eyes stare at you upside down.

I get positively angry with the impertinence of it and the everlastingness. Up and down and sideways they crawl, and those absurd, unblinking eyes are everywhere. There is one place where two breaths didn't match, and the eyes go all up and down the line, one a little higher than the other.

I never saw so much expression in an inanimate thing before, and we all know how much expression they have! I used to lie awake as a child and get more entertainment and terror out of blank walls and plain furniture than most children could find in a toy-store.

I remember what a kindly wink the knobs of our big, old bureau used to have, and there was one chair that always seemed like a strong friend.

I used to feel that if any of the other things looked too fierce I could always hop into that chair and be safe.

The furniture in this room is no worse than inharmonious, however, for we had to bring it all from downstairs. I suppose when this was used as a playroom they had to take the nursery things out, and no wonder! I never saw such ravages as the children have made here.

The wallpaper, as I said before, is torn off in spots, and it sticketh closer than a brother—they must have had perseverance as well as hatred.

Then the floor is scratched and gouged and splintered, the plaster itself is dug out here and there, and this great heavy bed, which is, all we found in the room, looks as if it had been through the wars.

But I don't mind it a bit—only the paper.

There comes John's sister. Such a dear girl as she is, and so careful of me! I must not let her find me writing.

She is a perfect and enthusiastic housekeeper, and hopes for no better profession. I verily believe she thinks it is the writing, which made me sick!

But I can write when she is out, and see her a long way off from these windows.

There is one that commands the road; a lovely shaded winding road, and one that just looks off over the country. A lovely country, too, full of great elms and velvet meadows.

This wallpaper has a kind of sub-pattern in a, different shade, a particularly irritating one, for you can only see it in certain lights, and not clearly then.

But in the places where it isn't faded and where the

sun is just sob—I can see a strange, provoking, formless sort of figure, that seems to skulk about behind that silly and conspicuous front design.

There's sister on the stairs!

Well, the Fourth of July is over! The people are all gone and I am tired out. John thought it might do me good to see a little company, so we just had mother and Nellie and the children down for a week.

Of course I didn't do a thing. Jennie sees to everything now.

But it tired me all the same.

John says if I don't pick up faster he shall send me to Weir Mitchell in the fall.

But I don't want to go there at all. I had a friend who was in his hands once, and she says he is just like John and my brother, only more so!

Besides, it is such an undertaking to go so far.

I don't feel as if it was worthwhile to turn my hand over for anything, and I'm getting dreadfully fretful and querulous.

I cry at nothing, and cry most of the time.

Of course I don't when John is here, or anybody else, but when I am alone.

And I am alone a good deal just now. John is kept in town very often by serious cases, and Jennie is good and lets me alone when I want her to.

So I walk a little in the garden or down that lovely lane, sit on the porch under the roses, and lie down up here a good deal.

I'm getting really fond of the room in spite of the wallpaper. Perhaps because of the wallpaper.

It dwells in my mind so!

I lie here on this great immovable bed—it is nailed down, I believe—and follow that pattern about by the hour. It is as good as gymnastics, I assure you. I start, we'll say, at the bottom, down in the corner over there where it has not been touched, and I determine for the thousandth time that I will follow that pointless pattern to some sort of a conclusion.

I know a little of the principle of design, and I know this thing was not arranged on any laws of radiation, or alternation, or repetition, or symmetry, or anything else that I ever heard of.

It is repeated, of course, by the breadths, but not otherwise.

Looked at in one way each breadth stands alone, the bloated curves and flourishes—a kind of "debased Romanesque" with delirium tremens—go waddling up and down in isolated columns of fatuity.

But, on the other hand, they connect diagonally, and the sprawling outlines run off in great slanting waves of optic horror, like a lot of wallowing seaweeds in full chase.

The whole thing goes horizontally, too, at least it seems so, and I exhaust myself in trying to distinguish the order of its going in that direction.

They have used a horizontal breadth for a frieze, and that adds wonderfully to the confusion.

There is one end of the room where it is almost intact, and there, when the crosslights fade and the low sun shines directly upon it, I can almost fancy radiation after all, the interminable grotesques seem to form around a common centre and rush off in headlong plunges of equal distraction.

It makes me tired to follow it. I will take a nap I guess.

I don't know why I should write this.

I don't want to.

I don't feel able. And I know John would think it absurd. But I must say what I feel and think in some way—it is such a relief!

But the effort is getting to be greater than the relief.

Half the time now I am awfully lazy, and lie down ever so much.

John says I mustn't lose my strength, and has me take cod liver oil and lots of tonics and things, to say nothing of ale and wine and rare meat.

Dear John! He loves me very dearly, and hates to have me sick. I tried to have a real earnest reasonable talk with him the other day, and tell him how I wish he would let me go and make a visit to Cousin Henry and Julia.

But he said I wasn't able to go, nor able to stand it after I got there; and I did not make out a very good case for myself, for I was crying before I had finished.

It is getting to be a great effort for me to think straight. Just this nervous weakness I suppose.

And dear John gathered me up in his arms, and just carried me upstairs and laid me on the bed, and sat by me and read to me till it tired my head.

He said I was his darling and his comfort and all he had, and that I must take care of myself for his sake, and keep well.

He says no one but myself can help me out of it, that I must use my will and self-control and not let any silly fancies run away with me.

There's one comfort, the baby is well and happy, and does not have to occupy this nursery with the horrid wallpaper.

If we had not used it, that blessed child would have! What a fortunate escape! Why, I wouldn't have a child of mine, an impressionable little thing; live in such a room for worlds.

I never thought of it before, but it is lucky that John kept me here after all, I can stand it so much easier than a baby, you see.

Of course I never mention it to them any more—I am too wise—but I keep watch of it all the same.

There are things in that paper that nobody knows but me, or ever will.

Behind that outside pattern the dim shapes get clearer every day.

It is always the same shape, only very numerous.

And it is like a woman stooping down and creeping about behind that pattern. I don't like it a bit. I wonder—I begin to think—I wish John would take me away from here!

It is so hard to talk with John about my case, because he is so wise, and because he loves me so.

But I tried it last night.

It was moonlight. The moon shines in all around just as the sun does.

I hate to see it sometimes, it creeps so slowly, and always comes in by one window or another.

John was asleep and I hated to waken him, so I kept still and watched the moonlight on that undulating wallpaper till I felt creepy.

The faint figure behind seemed to shake the pattern, just as if she wanted to get out.

I got up softly and went to feel and see if the paper did move, and when I came back John was awake.

"What is it, little girl?" he said. "Don't go walking about like that—you'll get cold."

I thought it was a good time to talk, so I told him that I really was not gaining here, and that I wished he would take me away.

"Why darling!" said he, "our lease will be up in three weeks, and I can't see how to leave before.

"The repairs are not done at home, and I cannot possibly leave town just now. Of course if you were in any danger, I could and would, but you really are better, dear, whether you can see it or not. I am a doctor, dear, and I know. You are gaining flesh and color, your appetite is better, I feel really much easier about you."

"I don't weigh a bit more," I said, "nor as much; and my appetite may be better in the evening when you are here, but it is worse in the morning when you are away!"

"Bless her little heart!" said he with a big hug, "she shall be as sick as she pleases! But now let's improve the shining hours by going to sleep, and talk about it in the morning!"

"And you won't go away?" I asked gloomily.

"Why, how can 1, dear? It is only three weeks more and then we will take a nice little trip of a few days while Jennie is getting the house ready. Really dear you are better!"

"Better in body perhaps—" I began, and stopped short, for he sat up straight and looked at me with such a stern, reproachful look that I could not say another word.

"My darling," said he, "I beg of you, for my sake and for our child's sake, as well as for your own, that you will never for one instant let that idea enter your mind! There is nothing so dangerous, so fascinating, to a temperament like yours. It is a false and foolish fancy. Can you not trust me as a physician when I tell you so?"

So of course I said no more on that score, and we went to sleep before long. He thought I was asleep first, but I wasn't, and lay there for hours trying to decide whether that front pattern and the back pattern really did move together or separately.

On a pattern like this, by daylight, there is a lack of sequence, a defiance of law, that is a constant irritant to a normal mind.

The color is hideous enough, and unreliable enough, and infuriating enough, but the pattern is torturing.

You think you have mastered it, but just as you get well underway in following, it turns a back somersault and there you are. It slaps you in the face, knocks you down, and tramples upon you. It is like a bad dream.

The outside pattern is a florid arabesque, reminding one of a fungus. If you can imagine a toadstool in joints, an interminable string of toadstools, budding and sprouting in endless convolutions—why, that is something like it.

That is, sometimes!

There is one marked peculiarity about this paper, a thing nobody seems to notice but myself, and that is that it changes as the light changes.

When the sun shoots in through the east window—I always watch for that first long, straight ray—it changes so quickly that I never can quite believe it.

That is why I watch it always.

By moonlight—the moon shines in all night when there is a moon—I wouldn't know it was the same paper.

At night in any kind of light, in twilight, candlelight, lamplight, and worst of all by moonlight, it becomes bars! The outside pattern I mean, and the woman behind it is as plain as can be.

I didn't realize for a long time what the thing was that showed behind, that dim sub-pattern, but now I am quite sure it is a woman.

By daylight she is subdued, quiet. I fancy it is the pattern that keeps her so still. It is so puzzling. It keeps me quiet by the hour.

I lie down ever so much now. John says it is good for me, and to sleep all I can.

Indeed he started the habit by making me lie down for an hour after each meal.

It is a very bad habit I am convinced, for you see I don't sleep.

And that cultivates deceit, for I don't tell them I'm awake—O no!

The fact is I am getting a little afraid of John.

He seems very queer sometimes, and even Jennie has an inexplicable look.

It strikes me occasionally, just as a scientific hypothesis—that perhaps it is the paper!

I have watched John when he did not know I was looking, and come into the room suddenly on the most innocent excuses, and I've caught him several times looking at the paper! And Jennie too. I caught Jennie with her hand on it once.

She didn't know I was in the room, and when I asked her in a quiet, a very quiet voice, with the most restrained manner possible, what she was doing with the paper—she turned around as if she had been caught stealing, and looked quite angry—asked me why I should frighten her so!

Then she said that the paper stained everything it touched, that she had found yellow smooches on all my clothes and John's, and she wished we would be more careful!

Did not that sound innocent? But I know she was studying that pattern, and I am determined that nobody shall find it out but myself!

Life is very much more exciting now than it used to be.

You see I have something more to expect, to look forward to, to watch. I really do eat better, and am more quiet than I was.

John is so pleased to see me improve! He laughed a little the other day, and said I seemed to be flourishing in spite of my wallpaper.

I turned it off with a laugh. I had no intention of telling him it was because of the wallpaper—he would make fun of me. He might even want to take me away.

I don't want to leave now until I have found it out. There is a week more, and I think that will be enough.

I'm feeling ever so much better! I don't sleep much at night, for it is so interesting to watch developments; but I sleep a good deal in the daytime.

In the daytime it is tiresome and perplexing.

There are always new shoots on the fungus, and new shades of yellow all over it. I cannot keep count of them, though I have tried conscientiously.

It is the strangest yellow, that wallpaper! It makes me think of all the yellow things I ever saw—not beautiful ones like buttercups, but old foul, bad yellow things.

But there is something else about that paper—the smell! I noticed it the moment we came into the room, but with so much air and sun it was not bad. Now we have had a week of fog and rain, and whether the windows are open or not, the smell is here.

It creeps all over the house.

I find it hovering in the dining room, skulking in the parlor, hiding in the hall, lying in wait for me on the stairs.

It gets into my hair.

Even when I go to ride, if I turn my head suddenly and surprise it—there is that smell!

Such a peculiar odor, too! I have spent hours in trying to analyze it, to find what it smelled like.

It is not bad, at first, and very gentle, but quite the subtlest, most enduring odor I ever met.

In this damp weather it is awful, I wake up in the night and find it hanging over me.

It used to disturb me at first. I thought seriously of burning the house—to reach the smell.

But now I am used to it. The only thing I can think of that it is like is the color of the paper! A yellow smell.

There is a very funny mark on this wall, low down, near the mopboard. A streak that runs round the room. It goes behind every piece of furniture, except the bed, a long, straight, even smooch, as if it had been rubbed over and over.

I wonder how it was done and who did it, and what they did it for. Round and round and round—round and round and round—it makes me dizzy!

I really have discovered something at last.

Through watching so much at night, when it changes so, I have finally found out.

The front pattern does move—and no wonder! The woman behind shakes it!

Sometimes I think there are a great many women behind, and sometimes only one, and she crawls around fast, and her crawling shakes it all over.

Then in the very bright spots she keeps still, and in the very shady spots she just takes hold of the bars and shakes them hard.

And she is all the time trying to climb through. But nobody could climb through that pattern—it strangles so; I think that is why it has so many heads.

They get through, and then the pattern strangles them off and turns them upside down, and makes their eyes white!

If those heads were covered or taken off it would not be half so bad.

I think that woman gets out in the daytime!

And I'll tell you why—privately—I've seen her!

I can see her out of every one of my windows!

It is the same woman, I know, for she is always creeping, and most women do not creep by daylight.

I see her on that long road under the trees, creeping along, and when a carriage comes she hides under the blackberry vines.

I don't blame her a bit. It must be very humiliating to be caught creeping by daylight!

I always lock the door when I creep by daylight. I can't do it at night, for I know John would suspect something at once.

And John is so queer now, that I don't want to irritate him. I wish he would take another room! Besides, I don't want anybody to get that woman out at night but myself.

I often wonder if I could see her out of all the windows at once.

But, turn as fast as I can, I can only see out of one at one time.

And though I always see her, she may be able to creep faster than I can turn!

I have watched her sometimes away off in the open country, creeping as fast as a cloud shadow in a high wind.

If only that top pattern could be gotten off from the under one! I mean to try it, little by little.

I have found out another funny thing, but I shan't tell it this time! It does not do to trust people too much.

There are only two more days to get this paper off, and I believe John is beginning to notice. I don't like the look in his eyes.

And I heard him ask Jennie a lot of professional questions about me. She had a very good report to give.

She said I slept a good deal in the daytime.

John knows I don't sleep very well at night, for all I'm so quiet!

He asked me all sorts of questions, too, and pretended to be very loving and kind.

As if I couldn't see through him!

Still, I don't wonder he acts so, sleeping under this paper for three months.

It only interests me, but I feel sure John and Jennie are secretly affected by it.

Hurrah! This is the last day, but it is enough. John to stay in town over night, and won't be out until this evening.

Jennie wanted to sleep with me—the sly thing! but I told her I should undoubtedly rest better for a night all alone.

That was clever, for really I wasn't alone a bit! As soon as it was moonlight and that poor thing began to crawl and shake the pattern, I got up and ran to help her.

I pulled and she shook, I shook and she pulled, and before morning we had peeled off yards of that paper.

A strip about as high as my head and half around the room.

And then when the sun came and that awful pattern began to laugh at me, I declared I would finish it today!

We go away tomorrow, and they are moving all my furniture down again to leave things as they were before.

Jennie looked at the wall in amazement, but I told her merrily that I did it out of pure spite at the vicious thing.

She laughed and said she wouldn't mind doing it herself, but I must not get tired.

How she betrayed herself that time!

But I am here, and no person touches this paper but me, not alive !

She tried to get me out of the room—it was too patent! But I said it was so quiet and empty and clean now that I believed I would lie down again and sleep all I could; and not to wake me even for dinner—I would call when I woke.

So now she is gone, and the servants are gone, and the things are gone, and there is nothing left but that great bedstead nailed down, with the canvas mattress we found on it.

We shall sleep downstairs tonight, and take the boat home tomorrow.

I quite enjoy the room, now it is bare again.

How those children did tear about here!

This bedstead is fairly gnawed!

But I must get to work.

I have locked the door and thrown the key down into the front path.

I don't want to go out, and I don't want to have anybody come in, till John comes.

I want to astonish him.

I've got a rope up here that even Jennie did not find. If that woman does get out, and tries to get away, I can tie her!

But I forgot I could not reach far without anything to stand on!

This bed will not move!

I tried to lift and push it until I was lame, and then I got so angry I bit off a little piece at one corner, but it hurt my teeth.

Then I peeled off all the paper I could reach standing on the floor. It sticks horribly and the pattern just enjoys it! All those strangled heads and bulbous eyes and waddling fungus growths just shriek with derision!

I am getting angry enough to do something desperate. To jump out of the window would be admirable exercise, but the bars are too strong even to try.

Besides I wouldn't do it. Of course not. I know well enough that a step like that is improper and might be misconstrued.

I don't like to look out of the windows even—there are so many of those creeping women, and they creep so fast.

I wonder if they all come out of that wallpaper as I did?

But I am securely fastened now by my well-hidden rope—you don't get me out in the road there!

I suppose I shall have to get back behind the pattern when it comes night, and that is hard!

It is so pleasant to be out in this great room and creep around as I please!

I don't want to go outside. I won't, even if Jennie asks me to.

For outside you have to creep on the ground, and everything is green instead of yellow.

But here I can creep smoothly on the floor, and my shoulder just fits in that long smooch around the wall, so I cannot lose my way.

Why there's John at the door!

It is no use, young man, you can't open it!

How he does call and pound!

Now he's crying for an axe.

It would be a shame to break down that beautiful door!

"John dear!" said I in the gentlest voice, "the key is down by the front steps, under a plantain leaf!"

That silenced him for a few moments.

Then he said, very quietly indeed, "Open the door, my darling!"

"I can't," said I. "The key is down by the front door under a plantain leaf!"

And then I said it again, several times, very gently and slowly, and said it so often that he had to go and see, and he got it of course, and came in. He stopped short by the door.

"What is the matter?" he cried. "For God's sake, what are you doing!"

I kept on creeping just the same, but I looked at him over my shoulder.

"I've got out at last," said I, "in spite of you and Jane. And I've pulled off most of the paper, so you can't put me back!"

Now why should that man have fainted? But he did, and right across my path by the wall, so that I had to creep over him every time!

The Were-Wolf

Clemence Housman

As she tugged at the door, he sprang across grasping his flask, but Sweyn dashed between, and caught him back irresistibly, so that a most frantic effort only availed to wrench one arm free. With that, on the impulse of sheer despair, he cast at her with all his force. The door swung behind her, and the flask flew into fragments against it. Then, as Sweyn's grasp slackened, and he met the questioning astonishment of surrounding faces, with a hoarse inarticulate cry: "God help us all!" he said. "She is a Were-Wolf."

Sweyn turned upon him, "Liar, coward!" and his hands gripped his brother's throat with deadly force, as though the spoken word could be killed so; and as Christian struggled, lifted him clear off his feet and flung him crashing backward. So furious was he, that, as his brother lay motionless, he stirred him roughly with his foot, till their mother came between, crying shame; and yet then he stood by, his teeth set, his brows knit, his hands clenched, ready to enforce silence again violently, as Christian rose staggering and bewildered.

But utter silence and submission were more than he expected, and turned his anger into contempt for one so easily cowed and held in subjection by mere force. "He is mad!" he said, turning on his heel as he spoke, so that he lost his mother's look of pained reproach at this sudden free utterance of what was a lurking dread within her.

Christian was too spent for the effort of speech. His hard-drawn breath laboured in great sobs; his limbs were powerless and unstrung in utter relax after hard service

Failure in his endeavour induced a stupor of misery and despair. In addition was the wretched humiliation of open violence and strife with his brother, and the distress of hearing misjudging contempt expressed without reserve; for he was aware that Sweyn had turned to allay the scared excitement half by imperious mastery, half by explanation and argument, that showed painful disregard of brotherly consideration. All this unkindness of his twin he charged upon the fell Thing who had wrought this their first dissension, and, ah! Most terrible thought, interposed between them so effectually, that Sweyn was wilfully blind and deaf on her account, resentful of interference, arbitrary beyond reason.

Dread and perplexity unfathomable darkened upon him; unshared, the burden was overwhelming: a foreboding of unspeakable calamity, based upon his ghastly discovery, bore down upon him, crushing out hope of power to withstand impending fate.

Sweyn the while was observant of his brother, despite the continual check of finding, turn and glance when he would, Christian's eyes always upon him, with a strange look of helpless distress, discomposing enough to the angry aggressor.

"Like a beaten dog!" he said to himself, rallying contempt to withstand compunction. Observation set him wondering on Christian's exhausted condition. The heavy labouring breath and the slack inert fall of the limbs told surely of unusual and prolonged exertion. And then why had close upon two hours' absence been followed by open hostility against White Fell?

Suddenly, the fragments of the flask giving a clue, he guessed all, and faced about to stare at his brother in amaze. He forgot that the motive scheme was against White Fell, demanding derision and resentment from him; that was swept out of remembrance by astonishment and admiration for the feat of speed and endurance. In eagerness to question he inclined to attempt a generous part and frankly offer to heal the breach; but Christian's depression and sad following gaze provoked him to self-justification by recalling the offence of that outrageous utterance against White Fell; and the impulse passed. Then other considerations counselled silence; and afterwards a humour possessed him to wait and see how Christian would find opportunity to proclaim his performance and establish the fact, without exciting ridicule on account of the absurdity of the errand.

This expectation remained unfulfilled. Christian never attempted the proud avowal that would have placed his feat on record to be told to the next generation.

That night Sweyn and his mother talked long and late together, shaping into certainty the suspicion that Christian's mind had lost its balance, and discussing the evident cause. For Sweyn, declaring his own love for White Fell, suggested that his unfortunate brother, with a like passion, they being twins in loves as in birth, had through jealousy and despair turned from love to hate, until reason failed at the strain, and a craze developed, which the malice and treachery of madness made a serious and dangerous force.

So Sweyn theorized, convincing himself as he spoke; convincing afterwards others who advanced doubts against White Fell; fettering his judgment by his advocacy, and by his staunch defense of her hurried flight silencing his own inner consciousness of the unaccountability of her action.

But a little time and Sweyn lost his vantage in the shock of a fresh horror at the homestead. Trella was no more, and her end a mystery. The poor old woman crawled out in a bright gleam to visit a bedridden gossip living beyond the fir-grove Under the trees she was last seen, halting for her companion, sent back for a forgotten present. Quick alarm sprang, calling every man to the search. Her stick was found among the brushwood only a few paces from the path, but no track or stain, for a gusty wind was sifting the snow from the branches, and hid all sign of how she came by her death.

So panic-stricken were the farm folk that none dared go singly on the search. Known danger could be braced, but not this stealthy Death that walked by day invisible, that cut off alike the child in his play and the aged woman so near to her quiet grave.

"Rol she kissed; Trella she kissed!" So rang Christian's frantic cry again and again, till Sweyn dragged him away and strove to keep him apart, albeit in his agony of grief and remorse he accused himself wildly as answerable for the tragedy, and gave clear proof that the charge of madness was well-founded, if strange looks and desperate, incoherent words were evidence enough.

But thenceforward all Sweyn's reasoning and mastery could not uphold White Fell above suspicion. He was not called upon to defend her from accusation when Christian had been brought to silence again; but he well knew the significance of this fact, that her name, formerly uttered freely and often, he never heard now: it was huddled away into whispers that he could not catch.

The passing of time did not sweep away the superstitious fears that Sweyn despised. He was angry and anxious; eager that White Fell should return, and, merely by her bright gracious presence, reinstate herself in favour; but doubtful if all his authority and example could keep from her notice an altered aspect of welcome; and he foresaw clearly that Christian would prove unmanageable, and might be capable of some dangerous outbreak.

For a time the twins' variance was marked, on Sweyn's part by an air of rigid indifference, on Christian's by heavy downcast silence, and a nervous apprehensive observation of his brother. Superadded to his remorse and foreboding, Sweyn's displeasure weighed upon him intolerably, and the remembrance of their violent rupture was a ceaseless misery. The elder brother, self-sufficient and insensitive, could little know how deeply his unkindness stabbed. A depth and force of affection such as Christian's was unknown to him. The loyal subservience that he could not appreciate had encouraged him to domineer; this strenuous opposition to his reason and will was accounted as furious malice, if not sheer insanity.

Christian's surveillance galled him incessantly, and embarrassment and danger he foresaw as the outcome.

Therefore, that suspicion might be lulled, he judged it wise to make overtures for peace. Most easily done. A little kindliness, a few evidences of consideration, a slight return of the old brotherly imperiousness, and Christian replied by a gratefulness and relief that might have touched him had he understood all, but instead, increased his secret contempt.

So successful was this finesse, that when, late on a day, a message summoning Christian to a distance was transmitted by Sweyn, no doubt of its genuineness occurred. When, his errand proved useless, he set out to return, mistake or misapprehension was all that he surmised. Not till he sighted the homestead, lying low between the night-grey snow ridges, did vivid recollection of the time when he had tracked that horror to the door rouse an intense dread, and with it a hardly defined suspicion.

His grasp tightened on the bear-spear that he carried as a staff; every sense was alert, every muscle strung; excitement urged him on, caution checked him, and the two governed his long stride, swiftly, noiselessly, to the climax he felt was at hand.

As he drew near to the outer gates, a light shadow stirred and went, as though the grey of the snow had taken detached motion. A darker shadow stayed and faced Christian, striking his life-blood chill with utmost despair.

Sweyn stood before him, and surely, the shadow that went was White Fell.

They had been together—close. Had she not been in his arms, near enough for lips to meet?

There was no moon, but the stars gave light enough to show that Sweyn's face was flushed and elate. The flush remained, though the expression changed quickly at sight of his brother. How, if Christian had seen all, should one of his frenzied outbursts be met and managed: by resolution? by indifference? He halted between the two, and as a result, he swaggered.

"White Fell?" questioned Christian, hoarse and breathless.

"Yes?"

Sweyn's answer was a query, with an intonation that implied he was clearing the ground for action.

From Christian came: "Have you kissed her?" like a

bolt direct, staggering Sweyn by its sheer prompt temerity.

He flushed yet darker, and yet half-smiled over this earnest of success he had won. Had there been really between himself and Christian the rivalry that he imagined, his face had enough of the insolence of triumph to exasperate jealous rage.

"You dare ask this!"

"Sweyn, O Sweyn, I must know! You have!"

The ring of despair and anguish in his tone angered Sweyn, misconstruing it. Jealousy urging to such presumption was intolerable.

"Mad fool!" he said, constraining himself no longer. "Win for yourself a woman to kiss. Leave mine without question. Such an one as I should desire to kiss is such an one as shall never allow a kiss to you."

Then Christian fully understood his supposition.

"I—I!" he cried. "White Fell—that deadly Thing! Sweyn, are you blind, mad? I would save you from her: a Were-Wolf!"

Sweyn maddened again at the accusation—a dastardly way of revenge, as he conceived; and instantly, for the second time, the brothers were at strife violently.

But Christian was now too desperate to be scrupulous; for a dim glimpse had shot a possibility into his mind, and to be free to follow it the striking of his brother was a necessity. Thank God! he was armed, and so Sweyn's equal.

Facing his assailant with the bear-spear, he struck up his arms, and with the butt end hit hard so that he fell. The matchless runner leapt away on the instant, to follow a forlorn hope. Sweyn, on regaining his feet, was as amazed as angry at this unaccountable flight. He knew in his heart that his brother was no coward, and that it was unlike him to shrink from an encounter because defeat was certain, and cruel humiliation from a vindictive victor probable. Of the uselessness of pursuit he was well aware: he must abide his chagrin, content to know that his time for advantage would come. Since White Fell had parted to the right, Christian to the left, the event of a sequent encounter did not occur to him. And now Christian, acting on the dim glimpse he had had, just as Sweyn turned upon him, of something that moved against the sky along the ridge behind the homestead, was staking his only hope on a chance, and his own superlative speed. If what he saw was really White Fell, he guessed she was bending her steps towards the open wastes; and there was just a possibility that, by a straight dash, and a desperate perilous leap over a sheer bluff, he might yet meet her or head her. And then: he had no further thought.

It was past, the quick, fierce race, and the chance of death at the leap; and he halted in a hollow to fetch his breath and to look: did she come? had she gone?

She came.

She came with a smooth, gliding, noiseless speed, that was neither walking nor running; her arms were folded in her furs that were drawn tight about her body; the white lappets from her head were wrapped and knotted closely beneath her face; her eyes were set on a far distance. So she went till the even sway of her going was startled to a pause by Christian.

"Fell!"

She drew a quick, sharp breath at the sound of her name thus mutilated, and faced Sweyn's brother. Her eyes glittered; her upper lip was lifted, and shewed the teeth. The half of her name, impressed with an ominous sense as uttered by him, warned her of the aspect of a deadly foe. Yet she cast loose her robes till they trailed ample, and spoke as a mild woman.

"What would you?"

Then Christian answered with his solemn dreadful accusation:

"You kissed Rol—and Rol is dead! You kissed Trella: she is dead! You have kissed Sweyn, my brother; but he shall not die!"

He added: "You may live till midnight."

The edge of the teeth and the glitter of the eyes stayed a moment, and her right hand also slid down to the axe haft. Then, without a word, she swerved from him, and sprang out and away swiftly over the snow.

And Christian sprang out and away, and followed her swiftly over the snow, keeping behind, but half-a-stride's length from her side.

So they went running together, silent, towards the vast wastes of snow, where no living thing but they two moved under the stars of night.

Never before had Christian so rejoiced in his powers.

The gift of speed, and the training of use and endurance were priceless to him now. Though midnight was hours away, he was confident that, go where that Fell Thing would, hasten as she would, she could not outstrip him nor escape from him. Then, when came the time for transformation, when the woman's form made no longer a shield against a man's hand, he could slay or be slain to save Sweyn. He had struck his dear brother in dire extremity, but he could not, though reason urged, strike a woman.

For one mile, for two miles they ran: White Fell ever foremost, Christian ever at equal distance from her side, so near that, now and again, her out-flying furs touched him. She spoke no word; nor he. She never turned her head to look at him, nor swerved to evade him; but, with set face looking forward, sped straight on, over rough, over smooth, aware of his nearness by the regular beat of his feet, and the sound of his breath behind.

In a while she quickened her pace. From the first, Christian had judged of her speed as admirable, yet with exulting security in his own excelling and enduring whatever her efforts. But, when the pace increased, he found himself put to the test as never had he been before in any race. Her feet, indeed, flew faster than his; it was only by his length of stride that he kept his place at her side. But his heart was high and resolute, and he did not fear failure yet.

So the desperate race flew on. Their feet struck up the powdery snow, their breath smoked into the sharp clear air, and they were gone before the air was cleared of snow and vapour. Now and then Christian glanced up to judge, by the rising of the stars, of the coming of midnight. So long—so long!

White Fell held on without slack. She, it was evident, with confidence in her speed proving matchless, as resolute to outrun her pursuer as he to endure till midnight and fulfill his purpose. And Christian held on, still self-assured. He could not fail; he would not fail. To avenge Rol and Trella was motive enough for him to do what man could do; but for Sweyn more. She had kissed Sweyn, but he should not die too: with Sweyn to save he could not fail.

Never before was such a race as this; no, not when in old Greece man and maid raced together with two fates at stake; for the hard running was sustained unabated, while star after star rose and went wheeling up towards midnight, for one hour, for two hours.

Then Christian saw and heard what shot him through with fear. Where a fringe of trees hung round a slope he saw something dark moving, and heard a yelp, followed by a full horrid cry, and the dark spread out upon the snow, a pack of wolves in pursuit.

Of the beasts alone he had little cause for fear; at the pace he held he could distance them, four-footed though they were. But of White Fell's wiles he had infinite apprehension, for how might she not avail herself of the savage jaws of these wolves, akin as they were to half her nature. She vouchsafed to them nor look nor sign; but Christian, on an impulse to assure himself that she should not escape him, caught and held the back-flung edge of her furs, running still.

She turned like a flash with a beastly snarl, teeth and eyes gleaming again. Her axe shone, on the upstroke, on the down stroke, as she hacked at his hand. She had lopped it off at the wrist, but that he parried with the bear-spear. Even then, she shore through the shaft and shattered the bones of the hand at the same blow, so that he loosed perforce.

Then again they raced on as before, Christian not losing a pace, though his left hand swung useless, bleeding and broken.

The snarl, indubitable, though modified from a woman's organs, the vicious fury revealed in teeth and eyes, the sharp arrogant pain of her maiming blow, caught away Christian's heed of the beasts behind, by striking into him close vivid realization of the infinitely greater danger that ran before him in that deadly Thing.

When he bethought him to look behind, lo! the pack had but reached their tracks, and instantly slunk aside, cowed; the yell of pursuit changing to yelps and whines. So abhorrent was that fell creature to beast as to man.

She had drawn her furs more closely to her, disposing them so that, instead of flying loose to her heels, no drapery hung lower than her knees, and this without a check to her wonderful speed, nor embarrassment by the cumbering of the folds. She held her head as before; her lips were firmly set, only the tense nostrils gave her breath; not a sign of distress witnessed to the long sustaining of that terrible speed.

But on Christian by now the strain was telling palpably. His head weighed heavy, and his breath came labouring in great sobs; the bear spear would have been a burden now. His heart was beating like a hammer, but such a dullness oppressed his brain, that it was only by degrees he could realize his helpless state; wounded and weaponless, chasing that terrible Thing, that was a fierce, desperate, axe-armed woman, except she should assume the beast with fangs yet more formidable.

And still the far slow stars went lingering nearly an hour from midnight.

So far was his brain astray that an impression took him that she was fleeing from the midnight stars, whose gain was by such slow degrees that a time equalling days and days had gone in the race round the northern circle of the world, and days and days as long might last before the end—except she slackened, or except he failed.

But he would not fail yet.

How long had he been praying so? He had started with a self-confidence and reliance that had felt no need for that aid; and now it seemed the only means by which to restrain his heart from swelling beyond the compass of his body, by which to cherish his brain from dwindling and shrivelling quite away.

Some sharp-toothed creature kept tearing and dragging on his maimed left hand; he never could see it, he could not shake it off; but he prayed it off at times.

The clear stars before him took to shuddering, and he knew why: they shuddered at sight of what was behind him. He had never divined before that strange things hid themselves from men under pretense of being snow-clad mounds or swaying trees; but now they came slipping out from their harmless covers to follow him, and mock at his impotence to make a kindred Thing resolve to truer form. He knew the air behind him was thronged; he heard the hum of innumerable murmurings together; but his eyes could never catch them, they were too swift and nimble. Yet he knew they were there, because, on a backward glance, he saw the snow mounds surge as they groveled flatlings out of sight; he saw the trees reel as they screwed themselves rigid past recognition among the boughs.

And after such glance the stars for awhile returned to steadfastness, and an infinite stretch of silence froze upon the chill grey world, only deranged by the swift even beat of the flying feet, and his own—slower from the longer stride, and the sound of his breath. And for some clear moments he knew that his only concern was, to sustain his speed regardless of pain and distress, to deny with every nerve he had her power to outstrip him or to widen the space between them, till the stars crept up to midnight. Then out again would come that crowd invisible, humming and hustling behind, dense and dark enough, he knew, to blot out the stars at his back, yet ever skipping and jerking from his sight.

A hideous check came to the race. White Fell swirled about and leapt to the right, and Christian, unprepared for so prompt a lurch, found close at his feet a deep pit yawning, and his own impetus past control. But he snatched at her as he bore past, clasping her right arm with his one whole hand, and the two swung together upon the brink.

And her straining away in self preservation was vigorous enough to counterbalance his headlong impulse, and brought them reeling together to safety.

Then, before he was verily sure that they were not to perish so, crashing down, he saw her gnashing in wild pale fury as she wrenched to be free; and since her right hand was in his grasp, used her axe left-handed, striking back at him.

The blow was effectual enough even so; his right arm dropped powerless, gashed, and with the lesser bone broken, that jarred with horrid pain when he let it swing as he leaped out again, and ran to recover the few feet she had gained from his pause at the shock.

The near escape and this new quick pain made again every faculty alive and intense. He knew that what he followed was most surely Death animate: wounded and helpless, he was utterly at her mercy if so she should realize and take action. Hopeless to avenge, hopeless to save, his very despair for Sweyn swept him on to follow, and follow, and precede the kiss-doomed to death. Could he yet fail to hunt that Thing past midnight, out of the womanly form alluring and treacherous, into lasting restraint of the bestial, which was the last shred of hope left from the confident purpose of the outset?

"Sweyn, Sweyn, O Sweyn!" He thought he was praying, though his heart wrung out nothing but this: "Sweyn, Sweyn, O Sweyn!"

The last hour from midnight had lost half its quarters, and the stars went lifting up the great minutes; and again his greatening heart, and his shrinking brain, and the sickening agony that swung at either side, conspired to appal the will that had only seeming empire over his feet.

Now White Fell's body was so closely enveloped that not a lap nor an edge flew free. She stretched forward strangely aslant, leaning from the upright poise of a runner. She cleared the ground at times by long bounds, gaining an increase of speed that Christian agonized to equal.

Because the stars pointed that the end was nearing, the black brood came behind again, and followed, noising. Ah! if they could but be kept quiet and still, nor slip their usual harmless masks to encourage with their interest the last speed of their most deadly congener. What shape had they? Should he ever know? If it were not that he was bound to compel the fell Thing that ran before him into her truer form, he might face about and follow them. No—no—not so; if he might do anything but what he did—race, race, and racing bear this agony, he would just stand still and die, to be quit of the pain of breathing.

He grew bewildered, uncertain of his own identity, doubting of his own true form. He could not be really a man, no more than that running Thing was really a woman; his real form was only hidden under embodiment of a man, but what it was he did not know. And Sweyn's real form he did not know. Sweyn lay fallen at his feet, where he had struck him down—his own brother—he: he stumbled over him, and had to overleap him and race harder because she who had kissed Sweyn leapt so fast. "Sweyn, Sweyn, O Sweyn!"

Why did the stars stop to shudder? Midnight else had surely come!

The Striding Place

Gertrude Atherton

Weigall, continental and detached, tired early of grouse-shooting. To stand propped against a sod fence while his host's workmen routed up the birds with long poles and drove them towards the waiting guns, made him feel himself a parody on the ancestors who had roamed the moors and forests of this West Riding of Yorkshire in hot pursuit of game worth the killing. But when in England in August he always accepted whatever proffered for the season, and invited his host to shoot pheasants on his estates in the South. The amusements of life, he argued, should be accepted with the same philosophy as its ills.

It had been a bad day. A heavy rain had made the moor so spongy that it fairly sprang beneath the feet. Whether or not the grouse had haunts of their own, wherein they were immune from rheumatism, the bag had been small. The women, too, were an unusually dull lot, with the exception of a new-minded débutante who bothered Weigall at dinner by demanding the verbal restoration of the vague paintings on the vaulted roof above them.

But it was no one of these things that sat on Weigall's mind as, when the other men went up to bed, he let himself out of the castle and sauntered down to the river. His intimate friend, the companion of his boyhood, the chum of his college days, his fellow-traveller in many lands, the man for whom he possessed stronger affection than for all men, had mysteriously disappeared two days ago, and his track might have sprung to the upper air for all trace he had left behind him. He had been a guest on the adjoining estate during the past week, shooting with the fervor of the true sportsman, making love in the intervals to Adeline Cavan, and apparently in the best of spirits. As far as was known there was nothing to lower his mental mercury, for his rent-roll was a large one, Miss Cavan blushed whenever he looked at her, and, being one of the best shots in England, he was never happier than in August. The suicide theory was preposterous, all agreed, and there was as little reason to believe him murdered. Nevertheless, he had walked out of March Abbey two nights ago without hat or overcoat, and had not been seen since.

The country was being patrolled night and day. A hundred keepers and workmen were beating the woods and poking the bogs on the moors, but as yet not so much as a handkerchief had been found.

Weigall did not believe for a moment that Wyatt Gifford was dead, and although it was impossible not to be affected by the general uneasiness, he was disposed to be more angry than frightened. At Cambridge Gifford had been an incorrigible practical joker, and by no means had outgrown the habit; it would be like him to cut across the country in his evening clothes, board a cattle-train, and amuse himself touching up the picture of the sensation in West Riding.

However, Weigall's affection for his friend was too deep to companion with tranquility in the present state of doubt, and, instead of going to bed early with the other men, he determined to walk until ready for sleep. He went down to the river and followed the path through the woods. There was no moon, but the stars sprinkled their cold light upon the pretty belt of water flowing placidly past wood and ruin, between green masses of overhanging rocks or sloping banks tangled with tree and shrub, leaping occasionally over stones with the harsh notes of an angry scold, to recover its equanimity the moment the way was clear again.

It was very dark in the depths where Weigall trod. He smiled as he recalled a remark of Gifford's: "An English wood is like a good many other things in life—very promising at a distance, but a hollow mockery when you get within. You see daylight on both sides, and the sun freckles the very bracken. Our woods need the night to make them seem what they ought to be—what they once were, before our ancestors' descendants demanded so much more money, in these so much more various days."

Weigall strolled along, smoking, and thinking of his friend, his pranks—many of which had done more credit to his imagination than this—and recalling conversations that had lasted the night through. Just before the end of the London season they had walked the streets one hot night after a party, discussing the various theories of the soul's destiny. That afternoon they had met at the coffin of a college friend whose mind had been a blank for the past three years. Some months previously they had called at the asylum to see him. His expression had been senile, his face imprinted with the record of debauchery. In death the face was placid, intelligent, without ignoble lineation—the face of the man they had known at college. Weigall and Gifford had had no time to comment there, and the afternoon and evening were full; but, coming forth from the house of festivity together, they had reverted almost at once to the topic.

"I cherish the theory," Gifford had said, "that the soul sometimes lingers in the body after death. During madness, of course, it is an impotent prisoner, albeit a conscious one. Fancy its agony, and its horror! What more natural than that, when the life-spark goes out, the tortured soul should take possession of the vacant skull and triumph once more for a few hours while old friends look their last? It has had time to repent while compelled to crouch and behold the result of its work, and it has shrived itself into a state of comparative purity.

If I had my way, I should stay inside my bones until the coffin had gone into its niche, that I might obviate for my poor old comrade the tragic impersonality of death. And I should like to see justice done to it, as it were—to see it lowered among its ancestors with the ceremony and solemnity that are its due. I am afraid that if I dissevered myself too quickly, I should yield to curiosity and hasten to investigate the mysteries of space."

"You believe in the soul as an independent entity, then— that it and the vital principle are not one and the same?"

"Absolutely. The body and soul are twins, life comrades—sometimes friends, sometimes enemies, but always loyal in the last instance. Some day, when I am tired of the world, I shall go to India and become a mahatma, solely for the pleasure of receiving proof during life of this independent relationship."

"Suppose you were not sealed up properly, and returned after one of your astral flights to find your earthly part unfit for habitation? It is an experiment I don't think I should care to try, unless even juggling with soul and flesh had palled."

"That would not be an uninteresting predicament. I should rather enjoy experimenting with broken machinery."

The high wild roar of water smote suddenly upon Weigall's ear and checked his memories. He left the wood and walked out on the huge slippery stones which nearly close the River Wharfe at this point, and watched the waters boil down into the narrow pass with their furious untiring energy. The black quiet of the woods rose high on either side. The stars seemed colder and whiter just above. On either hand the perspective of the river might have run into a rayless cavern. There was no lonelier spot in England, nor one that had the right to claim so many ghosts, if ghosts there were.

Weigall was not a coward, but he recalled uncomfortably the tales of those that had been done to death in the Strid. The practical Whitaker had disposed of Wordsworth's Boy of Egremond; but countless others, more venturesome than wise, had gone down into that narrow boiling course, never to appear in the still pool a few yards beyond. Below the great rocks, which form the walls of the Strid, was believed to be a natural vault, on to whose shelves the dead were drawn. The spot had an ugly fascination. Weigall stood, visioning skeletons, unconfined and green, the home of the eyeless things which had devoured all that had covered and filled that rattling symbol of man's mortality; then fell to wondering if any one had attempted to leap the Strid of late. It was covered with slime; he had never seen it look so treacherous.

He shuddered and turned away, impelled, despite his manhood, to flee the spot. As he did so, something tossing in the foam below the fall—something as white, yet independent of it—caught his eye and arrested his step. Then he saw that it was describing a contrary motion to the rushing water—an upward backward motion. Weigall stood rigid, breathless; he fancied he heard the crackling of his hair. Was that a hand? It thrust itself still higher above the boiling foam, turned sidewise, and four frantic fingers were distinctly visible against the black rock beyond.

Weigall's superstitious terror left him. A man was there, struggling to free himself from the suction beneath the Strid, swept down, doubtless, but a moment before his arrival, perhaps as he stood with his back to the current.

He stepped as close to the edge as he dared. The hand doubled as if in imprecation, shaking savagely in the face of that force which leaves its creatures to immutable law; then spread wide again, clutching, expanding, crying for help as audibly as the human voice.

Weigall dashed to the nearest tree, dragged and twisted off a branch with his strong arms, and returned as swiftly to the Strid. The hand was in the same place, still gesticulating as wildly; the body was undoubtedly caught in the rocks below, perhaps already halfway along one of those hideous shelves. Weigall let himself down upon a lower rock, braced his shoulder against the mass beside him, and then, leaning out over the water, thrust the branch into the hand. The fingers clutched it convulsively. Weigall tugged powerfully, his own feet dragged perilously near the edge. For a moment he produced no impression, then an arm shot above the waters.

The blood sprang to Weigall's head; he was choked with the impression that the Strid had him in her roaring hold, and he saw nothing. Then the mist cleared. The hand and arm were nearer, although the rest of the body was still concealed by the foam. Weigall peered out with distended eyes. The meager light revealed in the cuffs links of a peculiar device. The fingers clutching the branch were as familiar.

Weigall forgot the slippery stones, the terrible death if he stepped too far. He pulled with passionate will and muscle. Memories flung themselves into the hot light of his brain, trooping rapidly upon each other's heels, as in the thought of the drowning. Most of the pleasures of his life, good and bad, were identified in some way with this friend. Scenes of college days, of travel, where they had deliberately sought adventure and stood between one another and death upon more occasions than one, of hours of delightful companionship among the treasures of art, and others in the pursuit of pleasure, flashed like the changing particles of a kaleidoscope. Weigall had loved several women; but he would have flouted in these moments the thought that he had ever loved any woman as he loved Wyatt Gifford. There were so many charming women in the world, and in the thirty-two years of his life he had never known another man to whom he had cared to give his intimate friendship.

He threw himself on his face. His wrists were cracking; the skin was torn from his hands. The fingers still gripped the stick. There was life in them yet.

Suddenly something gave way. The hand swung about, tearing the branch from Weigall's grasp. The body had been liberated and flung outward, though still submerged by the foam and spray.

Weigall scrambled to his feet and sprang along the rocks, knowing that the danger from suction was over and that Gifford must be carried straight to the quiet pool. Gifford was a fish in the water and could live under it longer than most men. If he survived this, it would not be the first time that his pluck and science had saved him from drowning.

Weigall reached the pool. A man in his evening clothes floated on it, his face turned towards a projecting rock over which his arm had fallen, upholding the body. The hand that had held the branch hung limply over the rock, its white reflection visible in the black water. Weigall plunged into the shallow pool, lifted Gifford in his arms and returned to the bank. He laid the body down and threw off his coat that he might be the freer to practice the methods of resuscitation.

He was glad of the moment's respite. The valiant life in the man might have been exhausted in that last struggle. He had not dared to look at his face, to put his ear to the heart. The hesitation lasted but a moment. There was no time to lose.

He turned to his prostrate friend. As he did so, something strange and disagreeable smote his senses. For a half-moment he did not appreciate its nature. Then his teeth clacked together, his feet, his outstretched arms pointed towards the woods. But he sprang to the side of the man and bent down and peered into his face. There was no face.

Peregrine

Elinor Wylie

Liar and bragger,
He had no friend
Except a dagger
And a candle-end;
The one he read by,
The one scared cravens;
And he was fed by
The Prophet's ravens.
Such haughty creatures
Avoid the human;
They fondle nature's
Breast, not woman—
A she-wolf's puppies—
A wild-cat's pussy-fur:
Their stirrup-cup is
The pride of Lucifer.
A stick he carried,
Slept in a lean-to;
He'd never married
And he didn't mean to.
He'd tried religion
And found it pleasant;
He relished a pigeon
Stewed with a pheasant
In an iron kettle;
He built stone ovens;
He'd never settle
In any province.
He made pantries
Of Vaux and Arden,
And the village gentry's

Kitchen-garden.
Fruits within yards
Were his staples;
He drank whole vineyards
From Rome to Naples,
Then went to Brittany
For the cider.
He could sit any
Horse, a rider
Outstripping Cheiron's
Canter and gallop.
Pau's environs,
The pubs of Salop,
Wells and Bath inns,
Shared his pleasure
With taverns of Athens.
The Sultan's treasure
He'd seen in Turkey;
He'd known London
Bright and murky.
His bones were sunned on
Paris benches
Beset by sparrows;
Roman trenches,
Cave-men's barrows,
He liked, impartial;
He liked an Abbey.
His step was martial;
Spent and shabby
He wasn't broken;
A dozen lingoes
He must have spoken.
As a king goes
He went, not minding
That he lived seeking
And never finding.
He'd visit Peking

And then be gone soon
To the far Canaries;
He'd cross a monsoon
To chase vagaries.
He loved a city
And a street's alarums;
Parks were pretty
And so were bar-rooms.
He loved fiddles;
He talked with rustics;
Life was riddles
And queer acrostics.
His sins were serried,
His virtues garish;
His corpse was buried
In a country parish.
Before he went hence—
God knows where—
He spoke this sentence
With a princely air:
"The noose draws tighter;
This is the end;
I'm a good fighter
But a bad friend;
I've played the traitor
Over and over;
I'm a good hater
But a bad lover."